Contents Table

Section 6: Advanced Techniques

Section 7: Publishing & Maintenance

Section 8: Special Use Cases & Examples

Section 9: Inspiration & Next Steps

Appendices

- **Appendix A: Glossary of Key Carrd & Web Design Terms**
- **Appendix B: Quick Reference for Shortcuts & Settings**
- **Appendix C: Additional Design Resources & Tools**

~ Conclusion

Welcome & What You'll Learn

Welcome to **"The Carrd Handbook: Single-Page Websites in a Snap"**! Whether you're a complete beginner to web design or an experienced creator looking to streamline your process, this book is designed to provide a practical, no-nonsense guide to building stunning, responsive single-page websites using Carrd.

Why This Book?

In today's fast-paced digital world, single-page websites have emerged as one of the most effective tools for creating focused, visually appealing online experiences. Whether it's a personal portfolio, a product landing page, or an event announcement, single-page websites are often the perfect solution for delivering clear and concise content to your audience.

Carrd, with its intuitive no-code platform, empowers creators of all skill levels to bring their ideas to life quickly and effectively—without needing to write a single line of code. If you've ever felt intimidated by traditional web design platforms or found them overly complex for your needs, Carrd is the tool that can change how you think about website creation.

This book was written to help you unlock the full potential of Carrd, guiding you step by step through everything from the basics of setting up an account to advanced features like custom domains, SEO optimization, and user interaction enhancements.

What You'll Learn

By the end of this book, you will have:

1. **A Comprehensive Understanding of Carrd**
   - Learn how Carrd fits into the growing landscape of no-code tools and why it's uniquely positioned as a leading platform for single-page websites.
2. **Practical Design Skills**
   - Master essential design principles, including layout, typography, and color schemes, all within the Carrd platform.
3. **Hands-On Website Building**
   - Plan, create, and launch your very own single-page website from scratch, covering every step of the process.
4. **Advanced Techniques for Enhanced Functionality**
   - Explore advanced features like custom domains, embedding third-party widgets, and optimizing your site for performance and SEO.
5. **Insights into Special Use Cases**
   - Discover how to tailor Carrd to specific projects, from creating portfolio sites to monetizing your work with landing pages and newsletters.
6. **A Roadmap for Continued Growth**
   - Learn how to stay ahead of web design trends and leverage integrations and extensions for more complex projects.

How to Use This Book

This handbook is structured to serve both as a step-by-step guide for beginners and a reference manual for more experienced users. You can follow the chapters sequentially for a comprehensive learning experience or jump to specific sections that align with your immediate goals.

Here's how the content is organized:

- **Introduction:** Gain foundational knowledge about single-page websites, the no-code movement, and Carrd's core strengths.
- **Setting Up Your Workspace:** Learn how to navigate the Carrd platform, choose a subscription plan, and manage templates effectively.
- **Design Essentials:** Develop the skills needed to create visually appealing, responsive layouts.
- **Building Your Site:** Follow a detailed walkthrough of creating a functional single-page site, from planning to previewing.
- **Enhancing Interaction:** Add forms, buttons, navigation, and more to engage your visitors.
- **Advanced Features:** Explore professional-level tools like custom domains, analytics, and animations.
- **Publishing & Maintenance:** Understand the best practices for launching and maintaining your site.
- **Special Use Cases:** Learn how to adapt Carrd for diverse applications, including portfolios, landing pages, and more.

A Note on No-Code Tools

The rise of no-code platforms like Carrd represents a shift in how we approach website creation. You don't need to be a developer to create something beautiful and functional—what you need are the right tools and a clear understanding of how to use them effectively. This book aims to provide exactly that.

Your Next Steps

As you turn the pages of this book, you'll gain the confidence and skills needed to transform your ideas into reality with Carrd. So, get ready to dive in, explore, and create your first single-page website.

Let's begin this exciting journey together!

Section 1:
Introduction to Carrd and
Single-Page Websites

The Rise of Single-Page Websites

In the world of web design, trends evolve rapidly. Over the past decade, the rise of single-page websites has been one of the most transformative developments. These websites have redefined how businesses, individuals, and organizations communicate their message to users, emphasizing simplicity, speed, and clarity.

This chapter explores the factors driving the popularity of single-page websites, their defining characteristics, and why they've become a preferred choice for many projects.

What Are Single-Page Websites?

A single-page website, as the name implies, is a web design approach where all content is housed on one page. Instead of navigating through multiple pages, users scroll or use anchor links to jump to different sections of the same page. This design emphasizes a linear storytelling approach, ensuring that users receive a cohesive and uninterrupted experience.

The Evolution of Website Design

Traditionally, websites were built with multiple pages, each dedicated to a specific purpose—homepages, about pages, service pages, and contact pages, to name a few. While this approach remains useful for larger, content-heavy sites, it can be overkill for simpler needs, such as:

- **Portfolios**
- **Landing Pages**
- **Event Announcements**
- **Personal Branding Sites**

As mobile devices gained prominence, user behavior shifted. People began favoring quicker, more focused browsing experiences, making single-page websites an ideal solution.

Key Advantages of Single-Page Websites

Single-page websites have surged in popularity due to several compelling advantages:

1. **Enhanced User Experience (UX):**
   - Users appreciate seamless navigation and the ability to find all relevant information in one place.
   - Scrolling, particularly on mobile devices, has become second nature to users, making single-page designs intuitive.

2. **Focused Messaging:**
   - Single-page sites allow creators to present a clear, linear narrative without distractions, ensuring the main message stands out.
3. **Faster Load Times:**
   - Since all content resides on one page, there are fewer server requests, leading to faster load speeds—an essential factor for retaining visitors.
4. **Mobile Friendliness:**
   - With fewer navigation elements and streamlined layouts, single-page websites adapt well to smaller screens, enhancing usability.
5. **Simplicity in Maintenance:**
   - Updating or revising content is straightforward since everything is contained within a single file or project.

The Role of Technology

The rise of single-page websites can also be attributed to advancements in technology, such as:

- **Faster Internet Speeds:** Improved connectivity ensures smooth scrolling and quick loading of media-rich content.
- **Responsive Web Design Tools:** Platforms like Carrd make it easier than ever to create responsive single-page designs that work seamlessly across devices.
- **Enhanced JavaScript Libraries:** Tools like parallax scrolling and dynamic animations have added an interactive flair to single-page designs.

Popular Use Cases

Single-page websites excel in delivering concise, focused experiences. Some of the most common use cases include:

1. **Landing Pages for Marketing Campaigns:**
   - Perfect for product launches or lead generation, where the goal is to funnel users toward a specific action.
2. **Event Promotion:**
   - Provide all event details—location, schedule, and registration—in a single scrollable layout.
3. **Portfolios and Resumes:**
   - Showcase your work, skills, and achievements in a visually engaging format.
4. **Startup Pages:**
   - Offer a clear and compelling introduction to a product or service for startups.
5. **Personal Branding:**
   - Build a digital business card that highlights your expertise, personality, and contact information.

Challenges and Considerations

While single-page websites are advantageous, they are not without limitations:

1. **SEO Limitations:**
   - A single-page site may struggle to rank for multiple keywords compared to multi-page sites with dedicated content.
2. **Scalability Issues:**

- If your content grows significantly, you may need to transition to a multi-page layout.
3. **Performance Concerns:**
    - Media-heavy single-page designs can impact load times if not optimized properly.

By understanding these challenges, you can create solutions that maximize the effectiveness of your single-page website.

Why the Rise Matters

The popularity of single-page websites is more than just a trend—it reflects a broader shift in how users interact with online content. By prioritizing simplicity, clarity, and speed, single-page designs align with modern browsing habits.

With tools like Carrd making this approach accessible to everyone, now is the perfect time to explore how single-page websites can transform your digital presence.

Why Carrd Stands Out

The world of no-code web design is teeming with tools and platforms, each promising to simplify website creation. Yet, Carrd has emerged as a standout choice for creating single-page websites. Its blend of simplicity, versatility, and affordability has earned it a dedicated following among designers, entrepreneurs, and hobbyists alike.

This chapter delves into what makes Carrd unique, highlighting the key features and benefits that set it apart from other web design platforms.

Simplicity Without Compromise

Carrd's greatest strength lies in its simplicity. Unlike platforms designed to handle complex, multi-page websites, Carrd focuses exclusively on single-page designs. This specialization results in a user interface that is streamlined and intuitive, allowing even complete beginners to start building immediately.

Key Features of Carrd's Simplicity:

- **Drag-and-Drop Interface:** Move and resize elements effortlessly without any technical know-how.
- **Minimal Learning Curve:** Get up and running quickly, even if you've never built a website before.
- **Clutter-Free Dashboard:** Navigate easily with a design process that's focused and distraction-free.

Versatility for All Needs

Despite its simplicity, Carrd is incredibly versatile. It offers a range of features that allow users to build diverse types of websites. Whether you're creating a personal portfolio, a business landing page, or an event announcement, Carrd has the tools to bring your vision to life.

Examples of What You Can Build with Carrd:

1. **Landing Pages:** Generate leads, promote products, or drive conversions with sleek and effective layouts.
2. **Portfolios:** Showcase your work with customizable templates that highlight creativity and professionalism.
3. **Event Pages:** Share event details, RSVPs, and registration forms, all in one place.
4. **Personal Branding Sites:** Craft an online presence that reflects your personality and expertise.

Affordable and Accessible

Carrd's pricing model is another factor that sets it apart. Unlike many platforms that require expensive subscriptions, Carrd offers an affordable and transparent pricing structure:

- **Free Tier:** Build and publish a fully functional site without any cost.
- **Pro Plans:** Unlock advanced features like custom domains, third-party integrations, and higher file upload limits at an incredibly low price point.

This accessibility ensures that Carrd is within reach for everyone, from hobbyists to small business owners.

Mobile-First Design

In a world where mobile browsing dominates, Carrd shines by prioritizing responsive design. Every site you build on Carrd is optimized for mobile devices, ensuring that your content looks great and functions seamlessly, no matter the screen size.

Why Mobile Responsiveness Matters:

- **Enhanced User Experience:** Mobile-friendly designs improve navigation and readability for users on the go.
- **SEO Benefits:** Search engines favor websites that are optimized for mobile devices.

Intuitive Templates

Carrd's library of templates offers a starting point for users who may not know where to begin. These professionally designed templates cater to various use cases and are fully customizable, allowing you to adapt them to your specific needs.

Types of Templates Available:

- **Minimalist:** Clean and simple layouts for portfolios or personal branding.
- **Business-Oriented:** Professional designs tailored for landing pages and product showcases.
- **Creative:** Bold and colorful templates ideal for artists and designers.

Powerful Features for Advanced Users

While Carrd is beginner-friendly, it also caters to more advanced users who want to push the boundaries of single-page design.

Advanced Capabilities Include:

- **Custom Domains:** Establish a professional online presence with your own domain name.
- **Third-Party Integrations:** Embed forms, videos, and widgets from other platforms effortlessly.
- **SEO Tools:** Optimize metadata and content for better search engine visibility.
- **Analytics:** Track user behavior with built-in and third-party analytics tools.

A Community of Creators

Carrd's growing community of users is another reason it stands out. From design tips and template sharing to troubleshooting support, the Carrd community is a valuable resource for beginners and experts alike.

Benefits of the Community:

- **Inspiration:** Discover what others are building with Carrd.
- **Learning Resources:** Access tutorials, forums, and guides shared by users.
- **Support:** Get help and advice from a network of like-minded creators.

Why Choose Carrd?

Carrd's unique combination of simplicity, versatility, affordability, and advanced features makes it the ideal platform for anyone looking to create a single-page website. Whether you're a first-time builder or a seasoned designer, Carrd provides the tools you need to succeed without overwhelming complexity.

Understanding the No-Code Approach

The no-code movement is revolutionizing the way we build and interact with technology. It empowers individuals to create fully functional digital tools and platforms without needing to write a single line of code. Carrd is a prime example of this approach, offering an intuitive platform for creating professional single-page websites without requiring any prior technical expertise.

In this chapter, we'll dive into the fundamentals of the no-code approach, explore its benefits, and understand why it's become a game-changer for website creation.

What Is the No-Code Approach?

Traditionally, building websites or applications required extensive knowledge of programming languages such as HTML, CSS, and JavaScript. While coding skills remain valuable, the no-code approach eliminates this barrier by providing drag-and-drop interfaces, prebuilt templates, and user-friendly tools.

With platforms like Carrd, users can focus on the creative and functional aspects of their projects rather than the technical details, enabling faster and more accessible website creation for everyone.

The Core Principles of No-Code

The no-code approach is built on several key principles:

1. **Accessibility:**
   - Democratizing technology by making it accessible to non-technical users.
   - Enabling individuals and small businesses to create without relying on expensive developers.
2. **Simplicity:**
   - Using intuitive interfaces that minimize the learning curve.
   - Allowing users to focus on their goals without being bogged down by technical complexities.
3. **Speed:**
   - Reducing the time it takes to create, iterate, and publish digital projects.
   - Empowering users to move from concept to execution quickly.
4. **Flexibility:**
   - Providing tools and templates that can be customized to suit a variety of needs.
   - Allowing creators to adapt and refine their projects as they grow.

The Advantages of No-Code Platforms

No-code platforms like Carrd offer numerous advantages, making them an appealing choice for a wide range of users:

1. **Empowering Non-Developers:**
   - No-code tools remove the technical barriers, allowing anyone to bring their ideas to life.
   - This is especially beneficial for entrepreneurs, small business owners, and freelancers.
2. **Cost-Effectiveness:**
   - Eliminates the need to hire developers, saving significant time and money.
   - Offers affordable subscription models, such as Carrd's free and Pro plans.
3. **Rapid Prototyping:**
   - Enables users to test ideas quickly and iterate based on feedback.

      ○ Perfect for startups and creatives who need to validate concepts before scaling.
4. **Focus on Creativity:**
      ○ Frees users from technical challenges, allowing them to channel their energy into design and content.
      ○ Carrd's clean interface encourages experimentation and creativity.

How No-Code Is Changing Website Design

The no-code movement has fundamentally altered the landscape of web design. Platforms like Carrd are at the forefront of this change, enabling users to:

- **Build Responsive Websites:** Ensure designs look and function seamlessly across all devices.
- **Incorporate Advanced Features:** Add elements like forms, animations, and media without technical expertise.
- **Customize Designs:** Start with a template and make it uniquely yours through intuitive controls.

Who Benefits from No-Code Platforms?

The no-code approach is ideal for:

1. **Entrepreneurs:** Quickly launch landing pages or product showcases to test ideas and reach customers.
2. **Freelancers and Creatives:** Build portfolios or personal branding sites without outsourcing.
3. **Event Organizers:** Create single-page event websites with registration forms and schedules.
4. **Small Business Owners:** Establish an online presence without breaking the bank.
5. **Nonprofits and Educators:** Share information and resources with clean, user-friendly websites.

The Role of Carrd in the No-Code Revolution

Carrd epitomizes the no-code philosophy. It stands out for its simplicity, affordability, and versatility, making it an accessible entry point into website creation for users of all skill levels. With Carrd, you can:

- **Skip the Code:** Focus entirely on your project without worrying about technical details.
- **Create Quickly:** Go from idea to published site in hours, not days or weeks.
- **Experiment Freely:** Try different layouts, styles, and features without risk or frustration.

The Future of No-Code

The no-code movement is only gaining momentum. As tools like Carrd continue to evolve, they will empower even more creators to build digital solutions that were once out of reach. The rise of no-code is not about replacing developers but about complementing their work and enabling more people to participate in digital creation.

By embracing the no-code approach, you're joining a growing community of innovators who are shaping the future of web design and technology.

Pros & Cons of Single-Page Designs

Single-page websites have become a popular choice for designers, businesses, and individuals alike due to their simplicity, streamlined user experience, and adaptability. However, like any design approach, single-page websites come with their own set of strengths and limitations.

In this chapter, we'll explore the advantages and disadvantages of single-page designs to help you determine when this format is the right choice for your project.

The Pros of Single-Page Designs

1. Simplified User Experience (UX)

Single-page websites are designed for ease of navigation. Instead of clicking through multiple pages, users can access all the content they need by scrolling or using anchor links.

- **Benefit:** This streamlined experience keeps users engaged and minimizes the risk of them leaving due to confusion or frustration.
- **Best Use Cases:** Portfolios, landing pages, event announcements, and personal branding sites.

2. Clear and Focused Messaging

Single-page designs force creators to focus on the most important information and present it clearly.

- **Benefit:** A cohesive narrative guides users from start to finish without distractions.
- **Best Use Cases:** Product launches, sales funnels, and single-service websites.

3. Mobile Friendliness

With the rise of mobile browsing, single-page websites excel in providing a seamless experience on smaller screens.

- **Benefit:** Scrolling is more natural on mobile devices than clicking through multiple pages.
- **Best Use Cases:** Any site targeting mobile users or requiring responsive design.

4. Faster Development and Maintenance

Single-page websites are quicker to create and easier to maintain since all content is consolidated into one page.

- **Benefit:** Updates and revisions can be made without needing to navigate a complex site structure.
- **Best Use Cases:** Temporary campaigns, event websites, and prototyping.

5. Improved Conversion Rates

By focusing on one primary call-to-action (CTA), single-page designs often lead to higher conversion rates.

- **Benefit:** A single focus eliminates distractions and drives users toward a specific goal, such as signing up or making a purchase.
- **Best Use Cases:** Marketing campaigns, lead generation pages, and subscription forms.

The Cons of Single-Page Designs

1. Limited Scalability

Single-page websites are not ideal for projects requiring extensive content or multiple categories.

- **Challenge:** As content grows, the page can become cluttered, reducing usability and performance.
- **Example Issue:** An e-commerce site with dozens of products may not work well as a single page.

2. SEO Challenges

Multi-page websites have an advantage in search engine optimization (SEO) as they can target multiple keywords across different pages.

- **Challenge:** A single-page site can struggle to rank for diverse topics or keywords.
- **Solution:** Optimize your content with clear headings, meta descriptions, and focused keywords.

3. Performance Concerns

Media-heavy single-page designs can experience slow load times, particularly on mobile devices with slower connections.

- **Challenge:** Large images, videos, and animations can impact user experience.
- **Solution:** Optimize media files and implement lazy loading techniques to enhance performance.

4. Limited Analytics Insights

Single-page websites can make it difficult to gather detailed user behavior analytics.

- **Challenge:** You may only be able to track general site visits or clicks without understanding how users interact with individual sections.
- **Solution:** Use anchor link tracking or divide the page into segments in your analytics tool.

5. Potential Monotony

A single page with repetitive or poorly structured content can fail to hold users' attention.

- **Challenge:** Users may lose interest if the design lacks variation or creativity.
- **Solution:** Break up content with engaging visuals, animations, and clear section transitions.

When to Use Single-Page Designs

Single-page websites are ideal when:

- Your content is focused and doesn't require extensive subpages.
- You want to prioritize user experience and mobile responsiveness.
- Your project benefits from a linear narrative or call-to-action emphasis.
- You're working on a short-term campaign or event.

When to Avoid Single-Page Designs

Single-page websites may not be suitable if:

- Your project involves a large volume of content or multiple categories.
- SEO for multiple keywords or topics is a priority.
- You need detailed analytics insights into user behavior.
- The website's performance may be hindered by heavy media content.

Striking the Right Balance

While single-page designs excel in simplicity and focus, they are not a one-size-fits-all solution. Understanding the strengths and limitations of this format will help you make informed decisions about when and how to use it effectively.

Overview of This Book's Structure

Welcome to **"The Carrd Handbook: Single-Page Websites in a Snap"**! This chapter serves as your roadmap, guiding you through the book's layout and helping you understand how each section contributes to your journey of mastering Carrd and single-page website design. Whether you're a beginner eager to start from scratch or an experienced designer looking to refine your skills, this book is structured to cater to your needs.

How This Book Is Organized

The book is divided into **nine core sections**, each focusing on a specific aspect of working with Carrd and single-page website design. Let's explore what you can expect from each part:

Section 1: Introduction to Carrd and Single-Page Websites

This section lays the foundation by introducing you to single-page websites and the unique role Carrd plays in the no-code ecosystem. It answers key questions like:

- Why are single-page websites so popular?
- What makes Carrd an ideal tool for creating them?
- How does the no-code approach simplify web design?

You'll also explore the pros and cons of single-page designs to help you decide if this approach aligns with your project goals.

Section 2: Setting Up Your Carrd Environment

Before building your site, you need to understand the basics of the Carrd platform. This section covers:

- Creating your Carrd account and exploring the dashboard.
- Choosing a subscription plan that fits your needs.
- Working with templates and duplicating projects to save time.

By the end of this section, you'll have a fully functional workspace and the confidence to navigate Carrd's features.

Section 3: Design Essentials in Carrd

Design is at the heart of every successful website. This section focuses on:

- The fundamentals of layout, fonts, colors, and visual styles.
- Managing images, graphics, spacing, and alignment.
- Organizing your content with sections and containers.

These chapters ensure you have the tools to create visually appealing and well-structured designs.

Section 4: Building Your First Single-Page Site

Ready to start building? This section walks you through the step-by-step process of creating your first single-page website:

- Planning your site's structure and adding basic elements like text and images.
- Incorporating responsive design principles for mobile-friendly layouts.
- Adding backgrounds, media, and previewing your site before publishing.

This is where theory turns into practice, giving you hands-on experience.

Section 5: Enhancing User Interaction

A great website isn't just visually appealing—it's interactive and engaging. In this section, you'll learn to:

- Add navigation menus, anchor links, and contact forms.
- Embed videos, third-party widgets, and interactive buttons.
- Utilize tips and tricks to boost user engagement.

By the end, your site will not only look great but also function seamlessly to captivate your audience.

Section 6: Advanced Techniques

For those looking to take their skills to the next level, this section dives into advanced features:

- Setting up custom domains and optimizing your site for search engines.
- Adding tracking, analytics, scroll effects, and animations.
- Collaborating with teams and managing workflows efficiently.

These chapters are perfect for anyone aiming to create professional-grade websites.

Section 7: Publishing & Maintenance

Launching your website is just the beginning. This section covers:

- Testing and finalizing your site to ensure it's error-free.
- Publishing your website and making it live.
- Managing revisions, optimizing performance, and troubleshooting common issues.

You'll learn how to keep your site running smoothly after it's published.

Section 8: Special Use Cases & Examples

Carrd is a versatile tool that caters to various needs. This section explores real-world examples and specific use cases, such as:

- Creating landing pages, portfolios, and event pages.
- Building email capture forms and monetizing single-page websites.

These chapters inspire you to think creatively and apply Carrd to your unique projects.

Section 9: Inspiration & Next Steps

Stay ahead of the curve with insights into:

- Current web design trends and future possibilities with no-code tools.
- Integrations and extensions to expand Carrd's functionality.
- Comparing Carrd with other platforms and exploring the future of no-code design.

This section equips you with the knowledge to continue growing as a designer.

Additional Resources

To support your learning, this book also includes **three appendices**:

1. **Glossary of Key Terms:** Understand essential Carrd and web design terminology.
2. **Quick Reference Guide:** Access shortcuts and settings for faster workflows.
3. **Design Resources:** Explore tools, websites, and inspiration to enhance your skills.

How to Use This Book

This book is designed to be both a comprehensive guide and a quick reference manual. Here's how to make the most of it:

- **Beginners:** Start from the beginning and follow the chapters in sequence for a step-by-step learning experience.
- **Intermediate/Advanced Users:** Jump to specific sections or chapters that align with your goals.
- **Ongoing Reference:** Use the appendices and design resources to support your projects as needed.

By the end of this book, you'll have the skills and confidence to create stunning single-page websites using Carrd's no-code platform. Whether you're launching your first site or refining your expertise, this handbook is your go-to resource for mastering Carrd.

Section 2:
Setting Up Your Carrd Environment

Creating Your Carrd Account

Before you can dive into building stunning single-page websites with Carrd, you'll need to set up your account. Carrd's user-friendly onboarding process ensures that anyone, regardless of technical expertise, can get started in minutes. In this chapter, we'll guide you through the steps to create your Carrd account and explore some key features of the platform.

Why Create an Account?

While Carrd allows you to experiment with its tools without an account, creating one unlocks the full potential of the platform. With an account, you can:

- Save your projects and revisit them anytime.
- Access advanced features through Carrd's Pro plans.
- Manage your website settings, including publishing and revisions.

Creating an account is quick, free, and sets you on the path to mastering single-page website design.

Step-by-Step Guide to Creating Your Carrd Account

Follow these simple steps to create your Carrd account:

1. Visit the Carrd Website

- Open your preferred browser and go to https://carrd.co.
- On the homepage, you'll see an option to "Sign Up" in the top-right corner. Click on it to get started.

2. Enter Your Email Address

- Provide a valid email address. This will be used for account verification and communication.
- Make sure to use an email you check regularly, as important updates or password recovery emails will be sent here.

3. Choose a Password

- Create a strong, secure password for your account.
- Avoid using simple or common passwords for added security.

4. Agree to the Terms of Service

- Review Carrd's terms and conditions. Once you're comfortable, check the box to agree.

5. Submit Your Information

- Click the "Sign Up" button.

- You'll receive a confirmation email shortly.

6. Verify Your Email Address

- Open your email inbox and look for a message from Carrd.
- Click on the verification link in the email to activate your account.

Exploring Your Carrd Dashboard

Once your account is set up and verified, log in to explore Carrd's intuitive dashboard. Here's an overview of what you'll find:

1. Your Profile

- Access your account settings, including your email address, password, and subscription plan.

2. Create a New Site

- Start building your first site by selecting this option.
- You'll be guided to choose a template, but you can also begin with a blank canvas if you prefer complete customization.

3. Manage Your Projects

- View and edit all your saved projects.
- Organize your projects for easy access, especially if you're managing multiple sites.

4. Upgrade to Pro

- While Carrd's free version offers powerful features, upgrading to a Pro plan unlocks additional capabilities such as custom domains, larger file uploads, and integrations.

Troubleshooting Common Issues

Didn't Receive the Verification Email?

- Check your spam or junk folder, as automated emails may sometimes be filtered there.
- If you still don't see the email, click the "Resend Verification Email" option on the Carrd website.

Forgot Your Password?

- Use the "Forgot Password" option on the login page.
- Enter your registered email to receive instructions for resetting your password.

Technical Issues?

- Carrd's support team is available to help. Visit the "Help" section on the website for FAQs and contact options.

Tips for a Smooth Start

- **Bookmark the Carrd Website:** Save the URL for easy access.
- **Use a Strong Password Manager:** Secure your account details for added protection.

- **Familiarize Yourself with the Dashboard:** Spend a few minutes exploring the various tools and options available to you.

Creating your Carrd account is the first step in your journey to designing single-page websites effortlessly. With your account ready, you can now explore Carrd's features and start building.

Exploring the Dashboard

Once your Carrd account is set up, the next step is to familiarize yourself with its dashboard. The dashboard is where all the magic begins—it's your command center for creating, editing, managing, and publishing your single-page websites. Carrd's interface is clean, intuitive, and designed to make your workflow seamless, even if you're a first-time user.

This chapter provides a detailed walkthrough of Carrd's dashboard, highlighting its key features and functionalities.

Accessing the Dashboard

To access the dashboard:

1. Visit https://carrd.co.
2. Log in using your email and password.
3. Once logged in, you'll be taken to your dashboard.

Here, you'll see all your saved projects, access options to start new ones, and manage your account settings.

Key Elements of the Dashboard

Carrd's dashboard is designed for simplicity and efficiency. Let's explore its main components:

1. Your Projects Panel

- **Purpose:** Displays all the sites you've created and saved.
- **Features:**
  - **Project Thumbnails:** Each saved site is represented as a thumbnail, making it easy to identify.
  - **Quick Actions:** Hover over a thumbnail to edit, duplicate, or delete the site.
  - **Search Bar:** Use this to quickly locate a project if you have multiple sites.

2. Create New Site Button

- **Purpose:** This button lets you start building a new single-page website.
- **Features:**
  - When clicked, you'll be prompted to choose from Carrd's library of templates or start from scratch with a blank canvas.
  - Templates are categorized by purpose, such as portfolio, landing page, or personal branding, making it easier to find one that suits your needs.

3. Upgrade to Pro

- **Purpose:** Allows you to explore and activate Carrd's Pro features.
- **Features:**
  - Unlock advanced options like custom domains, form submissions, and third-party integrations.
  - View the details of various Pro plans and their benefits.

4. Account Settings

- **Purpose:** Manage your profile and subscription settings.
- **Features:**
  - **Profile Settings:** Update your email address, password, and other account details.
  - **Subscription Plan:** View or change your plan (free or Pro).
  - **Billing History:** Access your payment records if you've subscribed to a Pro plan.

Navigating the Dashboard

Carrd's dashboard is designed with simplicity in mind, but here are a few tips to make navigation even smoother:

1. **Organize Your Projects:**
   - If you're working on multiple sites, consider naming them descriptively so you can find them easily.
2. **Preview Thumbnails:**
   - Hover over project thumbnails to get a quick preview of each site without opening it.
3. **Sort and Filter:**
   - Use sorting and filtering options (if available) to group projects by date, type, or status.
4. **Explore Templates First:**
   - If you're new to Carrd, start by exploring its templates to understand the possibilities and structure of a single-page site.

Starting a New Site

To start building your first website, click on the **"Create New Site"** button. You'll be taken to the **template selection screen**, where you can choose from:

- **Category-Specific Templates:** Tailored designs for portfolios, businesses, events, and more.
- **Blank Canvas:** For users who prefer to start from scratch and customize every detail.

Once you select a template or blank canvas, you'll be taken to Carrd's editor, where you can begin customizing your site.

Benefits of the Dashboard

Carrd's dashboard is built to:

- **Save Time:** Quickly access and manage all your projects in one place.
- **Enhance Productivity:** Start new projects or edit existing ones with just a few clicks.
- **Keep You Organized:** Manage multiple sites without confusion.
- **Streamline Upgrades:** Easily explore and activate Pro features when needed.

Common Questions About the Dashboard

Can I Access My Dashboard on Mobile?

Yes! Carrd's dashboard is mobile-friendly, allowing you to manage your projects and make quick edits on the go.

What Happens If I Accidentally Delete a Project?

Deleted projects cannot be recovered, so double-check before confirming deletion.

How Do I Duplicate a Project?

Hover over the project thumbnail and click the "Duplicate" option. This is useful for creating similar sites or testing new ideas without affecting your original project.

Next Steps

Exploring the dashboard is the foundation for all your future work in Carrd. Spend some time getting comfortable with its layout and features. Once you're ready, move on to the next chapter, where we'll dive into **selecting a subscription plan** and understanding the benefits of upgrading to Pro.

Let's keep building!

Selecting a Subscription Plan

Carrd offers a range of subscription options to suit different needs and budgets. Whether you're a casual user exploring the platform for personal projects or a professional looking to unlock advanced features, understanding the available plans will help you choose the right one.

This chapter will guide you through the subscription plans offered by Carrd, their features, and how to select the best plan for your needs.

Overview of Carrd's Subscription Options

Carrd provides two primary types of plans: **Free** and **Pro**. Each plan caters to different levels of functionality and usage.

1. The Free Plan

- **Best For:** Beginners and casual users who want to experiment with Carrd.
- **Features:**
  - Create up to 3 sites for free.
  - Access to basic templates.
  - Publish sites with Carrd's branding in the URL (e.g., yoursite.carrd.co).
- **Limitations:**
  - No custom domains.
  - Limited features compared to Pro plans.
  - Branding appears on published sites.

The free plan is an excellent starting point, especially if you want to familiarize yourself with Carrd's capabilities before committing to a subscription.

---

2. The Pro Plans

Carrd offers three Pro plans that cater to different needs, each unlocking advanced features:

Pro Lite

- **Best For:** Individuals with simple projects who want a custom domain and no branding.
- **Features:**
  - Create up to 10 sites.
  - Use custom domains (e.g., www.yoursite.com).
  - Remove Carrd branding from your sites.
  - Access to premium templates.

Pro Standard

- **Best For:** Freelancers and small businesses managing multiple projects.
- **Features:**
  - Create up to 25 sites.
  - All features from Pro Lite.
  - Add forms with third-party integrations (e.g., email captures).
  - Larger file uploads for images and media.

Pro Plus

- **Best For:** Professionals and agencies handling numerous sites or complex projects.
- **Features:**
  - Create up to 100 sites.
  - All features from Pro Standard.
  - Advanced site elements (e.g., widgets, embeds, and animations).
  - Priority support for troubleshooting and inquiries.

How to Choose the Right Plan

Here's how to decide which subscription plan is best for your needs:

1. Evaluate Your Goals

- **Personal Projects or Experimentation:** Start with the free plan to explore Carrd's basic features.
- **Custom Branding and Domains:** Upgrade to Pro Lite for more professional-looking sites.
- **Business or Freelance Projects:** Pro Standard is ideal for managing multiple sites and integrating forms or widgets.
- **Large-Scale Projects or Agencies:** Pro Plus offers advanced features and higher limits, perfect for handling complex needs.

2. Consider Your Budget

- Carrd's Pro plans are competitively priced, offering excellent value for their features. Assess your budget and start with a plan that matches your current needs, upgrading later if necessary.

3. Start Small, Scale Up

- If you're unsure, begin with a lower-tier Pro plan. You can always upgrade as your projects grow.

How to Subscribe to a Pro Plan

Follow these steps to activate a Pro plan:

1. **Log in to Your Account**
   - Access your dashboard at https://carrd.co.
2. **Click "Upgrade to Pro"**
   - This option is visible on your dashboard.
3. **Choose Your Plan**
   - Review the features of each Pro plan and select the one that suits your needs.
4. **Enter Payment Details**
   - Carrd accepts major credit/debit cards for subscription payments.
5. **Complete the Transaction**
   - Once your payment is processed, your account will be upgraded instantly.

Benefits of Pro Plans

Upgrading to a Pro plan unlocks several advantages that elevate your Carrd experience:

- **Professional Websites:** Custom domains and branding-free designs enhance credibility.
- **Advanced Features:** Access to forms, widgets, analytics, and larger file uploads.
- **More Sites:** Manage multiple projects without limitations.

- **Priority Support:** Get help faster with Pro Plus.

Managing Your Subscription

Upgrading or Downgrading Plans

You can adjust your subscription at any time from the Account Settings in your dashboard.

Renewals and Cancellations

- Carrd subscriptions renew annually.
- If you decide to cancel, your Pro features will remain active until the end of the billing cycle.

Tracking Billing History

Access your billing history and invoices in the "Account Settings" section of your dashboard.

Conclusion

Selecting the right subscription plan is a crucial step in optimizing your Carrd experience. Whether you stick with the free plan or unlock the potential of Pro features, Carrd's flexibility ensures there's an option for everyone.

Working with Templates

Templates are one of the most powerful features of Carrd, providing a head start for your single-page website projects. Whether you're building a portfolio, landing page, or event site, Carrd's templates simplify the design process and help you create professional-looking websites in minutes.

In this chapter, we'll explore how to select, customize, and make the most of Carrd's templates.

What Are Carrd Templates?

Carrd templates are pre-designed layouts tailored for various purposes. They act as a starting point, providing a ready-made structure that you can customize to fit your specific needs. Templates are categorized by use case, such as personal branding, business, or events, and can save significant time compared to designing a site from scratch.

Benefits of Using Templates

Templates offer several advantages, particularly for beginners or those on tight deadlines:

1. **Time Efficiency:** Start with a functional layout and customize it, rather than creating a site from the ground up.
2. **Professional Design:** Templates are crafted by experienced designers, ensuring they follow best practices for usability and aesthetics.
3. **Inspiration:** If you're unsure how to organize your content, templates provide a clear structure to guide you.
4. **Customization Flexibility:** While templates provide a base, they're fully editable, allowing you to make them uniquely yours.

Types of Templates

Carrd offers templates for various use cases, ensuring there's something for everyone:

1. Personal Branding

- Ideal for resumes, portfolios, and personal introduction sites.
- Features: Simple layouts, sections for about, skills, and contact information.

2. Business and Landing Pages

- Tailored for startups, product launches, and lead generation.
- Features: Call-to-action buttons, service descriptions, and email capture forms.

3. Events and Announcements

- Perfect for promoting events, webinars, or gatherings.
- Features: Event details, RSVP forms, and countdown timers.

4. Creative Showcases

- Great for photographers, artists, and designers showcasing their work.
- Features: Image galleries, minimalist designs, and portfolio sections.

5. Blank Templates

- For those who want complete creative freedom.
- Features: A blank canvas to design your layout from scratch.

Selecting a Template

Follow these steps to choose a template for your project:

1. **Click "Create New Site"**
   - From the dashboard, select the "Create New Site" button.
2. **Browse Categories**
   - Templates are grouped into categories (e.g., Portfolio, Business). Browse through the categories that align with your goals.
3. **Preview Templates**
   - Hover over a template and click "Preview" to see how it looks and functions. Use this to evaluate if the template suits your needs.
4. **Select a Template**
   - Once you've found a template that fits your vision, click "Select." This will open the template in the Carrd editor for customization.

Customizing a Template

After selecting a template, you can customize it extensively to match your project requirements:

1. Editing Text and Images

- Replace placeholder text with your content.
- Upload your own images or select from Carrd's built-in image library.

2. Changing Colors and Fonts

- Adjust the template's color scheme to align with your branding.
- Choose from Carrd's font library or upload custom fonts (available with Pro plans).

3. Adding or Removing Elements

- Add new elements such as buttons, forms, or media blocks.
- Remove sections or elements you don't need to simplify the layout.

4. Rearranging Layouts

- Drag and drop elements to adjust their positioning.
- Use Carrd's alignment tools to ensure everything is perfectly arranged.

5. Testing Responsiveness

- Switch to mobile and tablet views in the editor to ensure your site looks great on all devices.

Tips for Working with Templates

1. **Start Simple:** If you're new to Carrd, choose a minimalist template to get comfortable with the editor.
2. **Save Progress:** Regularly save your project to avoid losing changes.
3. **Experiment:** Don't be afraid to modify templates. Use them as a guide but make them your own.
4. **Explore Premium Templates:** Pro users have access to a wider range of templates with advanced features and designs.

Frequently Asked Questions

Can I switch templates after starting a project?

No, Carrd does not allow template switching mid-project. If you want to use a different template, you'll need to start a new project.

Are templates mobile-friendly?

Yes, all Carrd templates are designed to be responsive, ensuring they look great on any device.

Can I use templates for free?

Yes, many templates are available for free. However, premium templates are exclusive to Pro users.

Conclusion

Templates are an invaluable tool in Carrd, helping you create stunning single-page websites quickly and efficiently. Whether you're a beginner looking for guidance or a pro seeking inspiration, templates provide the perfect starting point for your projects.

Importing & Duplicating Projects

As you work on multiple single-page websites in Carrd, you may find it helpful to reuse or build upon existing projects. Carrd makes this easy with its **importing** and **duplicating** features. Whether you're repurposing a template, creating variations of a site, or sharing your work with collaborators, these tools save time and streamline your workflow.

In this chapter, we'll explore how to import projects, duplicate existing sites, and leverage these features effectively.

Why Import and Duplicate Projects?

1. Save Time

- Instead of starting from scratch, import or duplicate a project to reuse existing layouts, styles, and elements.

2. Maintain Consistency

- Create multiple sites with a consistent design or structure, perfect for campaigns or branding.

3. Collaborate Easily

- Share project files with team members or clients, allowing them to review or edit the site.

4. Experiment Without Risk

- Duplicate a project to test new ideas or features without altering the original site.

Importing Projects

What Is Project Importing?

Project importing allows you to load a previously exported Carrd project file (.carrd) into your dashboard. This is particularly useful for sharing work or transferring projects between accounts.

How to Import a Project

1. **Access Your Dashboard**
   - Log in to your Carrd account and navigate to the dashboard.
2. **Click "Import Site"**
   - On the dashboard, locate and click the "Import Site" button.
3. **Upload the .carrd File**
   - Select the project file you want to import from your computer. Ensure it has the correct .carrd extension.
4. **Edit and Save**
   - Once imported, the project will open in the Carrd editor. Make any necessary edits and save the site to your dashboard.

Tips for Importing Projects

- Ensure the .carrd file was exported correctly from Carrd.

- Check for compatibility if the project uses Pro features (e.g., custom domains or forms) that require an upgraded plan.

Duplicating Projects

What Is Project Duplicating?

Duplicating creates an exact copy of an existing site within your dashboard. It's ideal for creating similar sites or experimenting with design changes.

How to Duplicate a Project

1. **Locate the Project**
   - In your dashboard, find the project you want to duplicate.
2. **Hover Over the Project Thumbnail**
   - Move your cursor over the thumbnail to reveal additional options.
3. **Click "Duplicate"**
   - Select the "Duplicate" option. A copy of the site will appear in your dashboard with the prefix "Copy of [Site Name]."
4. **Edit and Customize**
   - Open the duplicated site in the editor to make any changes or updates.

Benefits of Duplicating Projects

- **Create Variations:** Design multiple versions of a site to test different layouts or styles.
- **Manage Campaigns:** Use the same base design for multiple pages within a marketing campaign.
- **Backup Original Projects:** Duplicate a project before making major changes, ensuring you have a backup.

When to Use Importing vs. Duplicating

Feature	Best For
Importing	Sharing projects between accounts or transferring files from collaborators.
Duplicating	Creating similar sites or making edits without altering the original.

Common Scenarios

Scenario 1: Sharing a Project with a Client

You've designed a landing page for a client and need to share the editable file.

- Export the project as a .carrd file.
- Provide the file to your client for import into their Carrd account.

Scenario 2: Testing a New Feature

You want to add an advanced form to your site but aren't sure if it will work as intended.

- Duplicate the original project.

- Test the new feature on the duplicate without affecting the live version.

Scenario 3: Launching a Multi-Page Campaign

You're running a marketing campaign and need multiple landing pages with slight variations.

- Duplicate the base design.
- Customize each version with campaign-specific details.

Frequently Asked Questions

Can I import projects on a free plan?

Yes, you can import projects on the free plan. However, if the project includes Pro features (e.g., custom domains or forms), you'll need to upgrade to a Pro plan to use those elements.

Is there a limit to how many times I can duplicate a project?

No, you can duplicate a project as many times as needed, within the limits of your plan (e.g., number of sites allowed).

What happens if I import a project with Pro features into a free account?

The site will import successfully, but Pro-specific features will not function until you upgrade to a Pro plan.

Conclusion

Importing and duplicating projects are powerful tools for efficient website management in Carrd. These features save time, enhance collaboration, and provide flexibility for experimentation and growth.

Section 3:
Design Essentials in Carrd

Layout Fundamentals

The layout of a single-page website determines how content is organized and presented to visitors. A strong, well-structured layout not only improves user experience but also ensures that your message is conveyed effectively. In this chapter, we'll explore the fundamentals of designing layouts in Carrd, focusing on structure, balance, and usability.

What Is a Layout?

A layout is the arrangement of visual and textual elements on a webpage. In single-page websites, the layout is especially crucial because all content is displayed on one page, requiring careful organization to maintain clarity and flow.

Key considerations for a good layout:

- **Clarity:** The layout should guide users naturally through the content.
- **Visual Hierarchy:** Important elements, such as headings and calls to action, should stand out.
- **Responsiveness:** The layout must adapt seamlessly to different screen sizes.

Core Layout Elements in Carrd

Carrd provides a range of tools to help you structure your site effectively. Here are the core elements you'll use to build your layout:

1. Sections

- **Purpose:** Divide your site into distinct areas, such as an introduction, portfolio, or contact form.
- **How to Use:**
  - Add a new section in the Carrd editor.
  - Customize the section's background, spacing, and alignment.
- **Tip:** Use sections to create a natural flow for your content.

2. Containers

- **Purpose:** Group related elements together for better organization.
- **How to Use:**
  - Drag and drop elements (e.g., text, images) into a container.
  - Adjust the container's width, alignment, and background.
- **Tip:** Containers are great for maintaining consistent spacing and alignment across elements.

3. Grids and Columns

- **Purpose:** Create multi-column layouts for displaying content side by side.
- **How to Use:**

- ○ Use Carrd's grid settings to split a section into columns.
- ○ Add text, images, or other elements into each column.
- **Tip:** Use grids for comparison charts, team member profiles, or product features.

4. Spacers

- **Purpose:** Control the spacing between elements for a cleaner design.
- **How to Use:**
  - ○ Insert a spacer element where extra breathing room is needed.
- **Tip:** Use spacers to avoid clutter and improve readability.

Best Practices for Layout Design

1. Follow a Clear Visual Hierarchy

- Use larger fonts for headings and smaller fonts for body text.
- Place important elements, such as calls to action, in prominent positions.

2. Balance White Space

- White space (or negative space) refers to empty areas around elements.
- It improves readability and makes your site look more professional.

3. Prioritize Mobile Responsiveness

- Over 50% of web traffic comes from mobile devices.
- Use Carrd's responsive design tools to test your layout on different screen sizes.

4. Group Related Content

- Use containers or sections to group related elements, such as testimonials or services.
- This makes it easier for users to navigate your site.

5. Use Consistent Alignment

- Align text, images, and buttons consistently to create a polished look.
- Carrd's grid and alignment tools can help achieve this.

Example Layout Structures

1. Hero Section with Call-to-Action

- **Purpose:** Grab attention immediately.
- **Structure:**
  - ○ A bold heading.
  - ○ Supporting text with a brief introduction.
  - ○ A call-to-action button (e.g., "Learn More" or "Get Started").

2. Services or Features Section

- **Purpose:** Highlight what you offer.
- **Structure:**
  - ○ A heading for the section.
  - ○ Grid layout with icons and short descriptions for each service or feature.

3. Portfolio or Gallery Section

- **Purpose:** Showcase your work.
- **Structure:**
    - A heading (e.g., "Our Work" or "Portfolio").
    - Image grid or carousel with brief captions.

4. Contact Section

- **Purpose:** Make it easy for users to get in touch.
- **Structure:**
    - A heading (e.g., "Contact Us" or "Get in Touch").
    - A contact form or email link.
    - Optional: Social media links or a map.

Common Mistakes to Avoid

1. **Cluttered Design**
    - Overloading your layout with too many elements can overwhelm users.
    - **Solution:** Focus on simplicity and use white space effectively.
2. **Inconsistent Spacing**
    - Uneven gaps between elements can make your site look unpolished.
    - **Solution:** Use Carrd's alignment and spacer tools for consistent spacing.
3. **Ignoring Responsiveness**
    - A layout that looks great on desktop but breaks on mobile can frustrate users.
    - **Solution:** Test your design on multiple devices.
4. **Lack of Visual Hierarchy**
    - If all elements look the same, users won't know where to focus.
    - **Solution:** Use font sizes, colors, and spacing to establish a clear hierarchy.

Conclusion

Mastering layout fundamentals is key to creating visually appealing and user-friendly single-page websites. Carrd's intuitive tools make it easy to design layouts that guide users through your content effectively.

Fonts, Colors, and Visual Styles

Fonts, colors, and visual styles are the core elements that give your Carrd website its personality and appeal. By carefully selecting and combining these elements, you can create a design that not only looks great but also aligns with your brand and engages your audience.

In this chapter, we'll explore how to choose and customize fonts, colors, and visual styles in Carrd to make your single-page website visually striking and user-friendly.

Why Fonts, Colors, and Visual Styles Matter

1. First Impressions

- Fonts and colors are among the first things visitors notice. They set the tone for your site and create an immediate impression.

2. Branding and Consistency

- A cohesive visual style helps establish your brand's identity and makes your site memorable.

3. Usability and Readability

- Thoughtful font and color choices improve readability and ensure that your content is accessible to all users.

Working with Fonts

Choosing the Right Font

Carrd offers a selection of fonts suitable for various purposes. When selecting a font, consider:

- **Readability:** Ensure that body text is legible on all devices.
- **Tone:** Use fonts that match the mood of your website (e.g., playful, professional, modern).
- **Consistency:** Stick to one or two fonts to avoid visual clutter.

How to Customize Fonts in Carrd

1. **Open the Editor:** Navigate to the section or element where you want to change the font.
2. **Select the Font Option:** In the style settings, locate the font dropdown menu.
3. **Choose a Font:** Pick from Carrd's library of built-in fonts.
4. **Adjust Font Size and Weight:**
   - Increase the size for headings and reduce it for body text.
   - Use bold or regular weights to emphasize key points.
5. **Add Custom Fonts (Pro Feature):**
   - If you're on a Pro plan, you can upload custom fonts to further personalize your site.

Font Pairing Tips

- **Heading and Body Text:** Pair a decorative font for headings with a clean sans-serif font for body text.
- **Avoid Overuse:** Limit your font choices to maintain a professional look.

Choosing Colors

The Basics of Color Theory

Understanding basic color theory helps you create harmonious and visually appealing designs:

- **Primary Colors:** Red, blue, and yellow are the foundation of all other colors.
- **Complementary Colors:** Colors opposite each other on the color wheel create contrast (e.g., blue and orange).
- **Analogous Colors:** Colors next to each other on the wheel create a cohesive, calming effect (e.g., green and yellow-green).

Using Colors in Carrd

1. **Select the Element:** Open the style settings for the section, text, or button you want to customize.
2. **Choose a Color:** Use the color picker to select your desired shade.
3. **Use Hex Codes:** If you have a specific color in mind, enter its hex code for precision.
4. **Apply Gradients (Pro Feature):** Create dynamic backgrounds or buttons using gradient options available in Pro plans.

Tips for Effective Color Use

- **Stick to a Palette:** Use 3-5 colors to maintain consistency.
- **Prioritize Contrast:** Ensure there's enough contrast between text and background for readability.
- **Test on Devices:** Check how colors appear on different screens and lighting conditions.

Accessibility Considerations

- Use tools like contrast checkers to ensure your color choices meet accessibility standards.
- Avoid relying solely on color to convey meaning (e.g., use labels or icons in addition to color).

Applying Visual Styles

Visual styles include effects like borders, shadows, and background patterns that add depth and polish to your design.

How to Add Visual Styles in Carrd

1. **Borders:**
   - Apply borders to sections or containers to define areas.
   - Adjust thickness and color for subtle or bold effects.
2. **Shadows:**
   - Use drop shadows to add depth to text, buttons, or images.
   - Keep shadows minimal for a modern, clean look.
3. **Backgrounds:**
   - Set solid colors, gradients, or images as section backgrounds.
   - Use texture or patterns to add visual interest.
4. **Hover Effects:**
   - Add hover effects to buttons or links for interactivity (e.g., color changes, shadows).

Examples of Effective Styles

1. Minimalist Design

- **Fonts:** Clean sans-serif fonts for headings and body text.
- **Colors:** Neutral tones (white, gray) with a single accent color.
- **Styles:** Subtle shadows and borders for depth.

2. Bold and Vibrant Design

- **Fonts:** Modern or decorative fonts for headings.
- **Colors:** Bright, contrasting colors for energy.
- **Styles:** Gradient backgrounds and bold hover effects.

3. Professional and Corporate Design

- **Fonts:** Serif fonts for headings, sans-serif for body text.
- **Colors:** Blues and grays with a pop of warm color.
- **Styles:** Minimal effects with clean lines and defined sections.

Common Mistakes to Avoid

1. **Overloading with Fonts:** Too many font styles can make your site look chaotic.
2. **Inconsistent Colors:** Mismatched colors can confuse or overwhelm visitors.
3. **Excessive Effects:** Overusing shadows or hover effects can distract from content.
4. **Ignoring Accessibility:** Low contrast or illegible fonts can alienate users.

Conclusion

Fonts, colors, and visual styles are the building blocks of a compelling website. With Carrd's tools, you can experiment and refine these elements to create a site that reflects your brand and engages your audience.

Managing Images & Graphics

Images and graphics are essential components of any website. They grab attention, convey information quickly, and enhance the overall visual appeal of your design. Carrd makes it easy to add, edit, and optimize images to create a professional-looking single-page website.

In this chapter, we'll explore how to manage images and graphics in Carrd, covering everything from uploading and customizing to ensuring optimal performance.

The Role of Images in Website Design

Why Images Matter

1. **Visual Appeal:** Images break up text-heavy sections and make your site visually engaging.
2. **Storytelling:** Pictures can communicate ideas and emotions more effectively than text alone.
3. **Brand Identity:** Graphics and images reinforce your brand's personality and message.

Common Use Cases

- **Hero Images:** Large, impactful images at the top of your site.
- **Portfolios:** Displaying your work or projects.
- **Product Photos:** Showcasing items for e-commerce or marketing.
- **Backgrounds:** Adding texture and depth to sections.

Adding Images to Your Carrd Site

How to Add an Image

1. **Open the Carrd Editor:** Navigate to the section where you want to add an image.
2. **Click "+" to Add an Element:** Select "Image" from the list of available elements.
3. **Upload Your Image:** Choose an image from your computer or drag and drop it into the upload box.
4. **Position and Resize:** Use the drag handles to adjust the image's size and placement.

Using Image Links

- Instead of uploading, you can link to an image hosted online by entering its URL.

Customizing Images

Carrd provides several customization options to ensure your images fit seamlessly into your design:

1. Adjusting Dimensions

- Resize images directly in the editor using the drag handles.
- For precise dimensions, enter specific height and width values in the settings panel.

2. Adding Borders and Shadows

- Add borders to give images a framed appearance.
- Apply shadows to add depth and make images stand out.

3. Cropping and Alignment

- Crop images to focus on specific areas.
- Align images left, center, or right to create a balanced layout.

4. Alt Text (Pro Feature)

- Add alt text to images to improve accessibility and SEO.
- Describe the content of the image in concise, meaningful terms.

Background Images

How to Use Background Images

1. **Select a Section:** Open the settings for the section you want to customize.
2. **Choose Background Type:** Set the background to "Image."
3. **Upload or Link an Image:** Add your desired image.
4. **Adjust Settings:**
   - **Position:** Center, top, bottom, etc.
   - **Size:** Cover, contain, or custom dimensions.
   - **Overlay:** Add a color overlay for better text readability.

Best Practices for Background Images

- Use high-resolution images for a polished look.
- Ensure text placed over the background is easily readable (use overlays if needed).
- Test how the image appears on different screen sizes.

Optimizing Images for Performance

Why Optimization Matters

Large image files can slow down your website, leading to poor user experience and lower search engine rankings.

Tips for Optimization

1. **Resize Before Uploading:** Use image editing tools to resize images to the dimensions needed for your site.
2. **Compress Images:** Reduce file size without sacrificing quality using tools like TinyPNG or JPEG Optimizer.
3. **Use Appropriate File Formats:**
   - **JPEG:** Best for photos and images with many colors.
   - **PNG:** Best for graphics with transparency or text overlays.
   - **SVG:** Best for icons and vector graphics.
4. **Lazy Loading (Pro Feature):** Enable lazy loading to delay image loading until they're visible on the screen, improving initial page load speed.

Adding Graphics and Icons

Using Custom Graphics

- Upload your own graphics, such as logos or illustrations, to personalize your site.
- Ensure graphics are saved in the appropriate format (e.g., PNG for transparency).

Using Built-In Icons (Pro Feature)

Carrd offers a library of icons for quick and easy customization:

1. Add an icon element from the editor.
2. Browse or search the icon library.
3. Customize size, color, and alignment.

Common Mistakes to Avoid

1. **Overusing Images:** Too many images can clutter your design and distract from your content.
2. **Poor Quality:** Blurry or pixelated images reduce professionalism. Always use high-quality visuals.
3. **Ignoring Accessibility:** Failing to add alt text makes your site less inclusive and hurts SEO.
4. **Slow Load Times:** Large image files can frustrate users and affect site performance. Always optimize.

Conclusion

Images and graphics play a crucial role in the design and functionality of your Carrd website. By managing these elements effectively, you can create visually appealing, fast-loading, and user-friendly sites that leave a lasting impression on your audience.

Spacing & Alignment

Spacing and alignment are the unsung heroes of great design. They might not seem as exciting as fonts or colors, but they play a vital role in making your Carrd website clean, professional, and easy to navigate. Poor spacing and alignment can make even the most beautiful designs look cluttered or disorganized, while thoughtful use of these elements can elevate your website to the next level.

In this chapter, we'll explore how to use spacing and alignment tools in Carrd to create a balanced and visually pleasing layout.

Why Spacing and Alignment Matter

1. Readability and Clarity

Proper spacing makes content easier to read and understand, ensuring visitors can quickly grasp your message.

2. Visual Balance

Balanced spacing and alignment create harmony in your design, making it more appealing to the eye.

3. Focus and Emphasis

Strategic use of spacing directs attention to key elements, such as headings, images, or calls to action.

4. Professionalism

A well-aligned layout signals attention to detail and makes your site appear more polished and credible.

Understanding Spacing in Carrd

Types of Spacing

1. **Element Spacing:** The distance between individual elements (e.g., text, buttons, images).
2. **Section Spacing:** The padding and margins around sections or containers.
3. **Line Spacing:** The vertical space between lines of text.

How to Adjust Spacing

1. **Select an Element or Section**
   - Click on the element or section you want to adjust.
2. **Open the Style Settings**
   - Navigate to the "Spacing" or "Padding/Margin" options.
3. **Adjust Padding and Margins**
   - **Padding:** Controls the space inside an element or section.
   - **Margin:** Controls the space outside an element or section.
4. **Use Spacers**
   - Add spacer elements to create custom gaps between sections or elements.

Tips for Effective Spacing

- Maintain consistent spacing throughout your site for a cohesive look.
- Use larger spacing around important elements to make them stand out.

- Avoid crowding elements together; give them room to breathe.

Aligning Elements in Carrd

Types of Alignment

1. **Horizontal Alignment:** Align elements to the left, center, or right of a section or container.
2. **Vertical Alignment:** Align elements to the top, middle, or bottom of a section or container.

How to Align Elements

1. **Select the Element**
   - Click on the element you want to align.
2. **Open the Style Settings**
   - Navigate to the "Alignment" or "Position" options.
3. **Choose an Alignment Option**
   - Horizontal: Align left, center, or right.
   - Vertical: Align top, middle, or bottom.
4. **Use Containers for Group Alignment**
   - Place related elements in a container and align the container as a whole.

Tips for Effective Alignment

- Center align key content like headlines or calls to action to draw attention.
- Use left alignment for body text to improve readability.
- Align elements consistently within a section to avoid a disorganized look.

Using Grids for Precision

Grids are a powerful tool for maintaining consistent alignment and spacing:

1. **Enable Gridlines**
   - Use the gridlines option in the Carrd editor to align elements precisely.
2. **Snap to Grid**
   - Enable snapping to automatically align elements with the gridlines.
3. **Divide Sections into Columns**
   - Use multiple columns to organize content side by side (e.g., text and images).

Benefits of Using Grids

- Ensures a professional, balanced layout.
- Simplifies alignment across sections.
- Speeds up the design process.

Common Mistakes to Avoid

1. **Inconsistent Spacing**
   - Uneven gaps between elements can make your site look unpolished.
   - **Solution:** Use Carrd's padding and margin tools for consistency.
2. **Overcrowding**
   - Placing too many elements close together creates visual clutter.

       ○ **Solution:** Use spacers and generous padding to give elements breathing room.

3. **Misaligned Elements**
   - Misalignment disrupts the flow of your design.
   - **Solution:** Use Carrd's gridlines and alignment tools for precision.
4. **Neglecting Mobile Alignment**
   - Elements that look aligned on desktop may appear misaligned on mobile.
   - **Solution:** Test your site on multiple devices to ensure alignment is consistent.

Examples of Good Spacing and Alignment

1. Hero Section

- Large heading centered vertically and horizontally.
- Ample spacing above and below the call-to-action button.

2. Service Section

- Grid layout with equal spacing between service cards.
- Consistent padding within each card for text and icons.

3. Contact Section

- Form fields aligned vertically with equal spacing between them.
- Submit button centered below the form.

Conclusion

Mastering spacing and alignment is crucial for creating clean, professional, and visually appealing Carrd websites. With Carrd's intuitive tools, you can fine-tune these elements to enhance readability, balance, and focus in your designs.

Sections, Containers & Organization

Effective organization is the backbone of any great single-page website. In Carrd, **sections** and **containers** are the primary tools for structuring your content. They help create a logical flow, group related elements, and ensure a seamless user experience. In this chapter, we'll explore how to use sections and containers effectively, and how to organize your content for maximum impact.

Understanding Sections

What Are Sections?

Sections are the building blocks of your Carrd site. They divide your website into distinct areas, such as a hero banner, services, testimonials, or a contact form.

Why Use Sections?

- **Clarity:** Sections make it easy for visitors to understand your site at a glance.
- **Design Flexibility:** Each section can have unique styling, backgrounds, and spacing.
- **Navigation:** Sections enable anchor links, which let users jump directly to specific parts of your site.

How to Add a Section

1. **Open the Carrd Editor:** Start by accessing your project in the editor.
2. **Click "+" to Add a Section:** Choose "Section" from the elements list.
3. **Customize the Section:** Adjust the section's settings, including:
   - **Background:** Choose a color, gradient, or image.
   - **Padding:** Control the spacing inside the section.
   - **Alignment:** Center, left, or right align the content.

Best Practices for Sections

1. **One Purpose per Section:** Keep each section focused on a single topic, such as a call to action or a portfolio.
2. **Visual Separation:** Use contrasting backgrounds or ample spacing to distinguish one section from the next.
3. **Logical Order:** Arrange sections in a flow that aligns with your goals (e.g., introduction, features, testimonials, contact).

Exploring Containers

What Are Containers?

Containers are flexible tools for grouping elements within a section. They're ideal for organizing related items, such as text and images, in a clean and cohesive way.

Why Use Containers?

- **Consistency:** Ensure elements are aligned and spaced uniformly.
- **Flexibility:** Move groups of elements together without affecting the rest of the layout.
- **Customization:** Apply unique styling to a group of elements without altering the entire section.

How to Add a Container

1. **Open a Section:** Select the section where you want to add a container.
2. **Click "+" to Add a Container:** Choose "Container" from the elements list.
3. **Drag Elements into the Container:** Add text, buttons, images, or other elements into the container.

Customizing Containers

- **Width:** Adjust the container's width to control how much space it occupies.
- **Padding and Margins:** Add spacing inside and around the container.
- **Background:** Set a background color, gradient, or image for the container.
- **Borders and Shadows:** Use borders or shadows to visually separate the container from the rest of the section.

Organizing Content Effectively

Grouping Related Elements

- Use containers to group related items, such as a heading, subheading, and button.
- Keep elements that serve the same purpose in close proximity for clarity.

Creating Visual Hierarchy

- Place the most important elements (e.g., headlines, calls to action) at the top of sections.
- Use font sizes, colors, and spacing to guide users through the content.

Maintaining Consistency

- Apply consistent padding, margins, and alignment across sections and containers.
- Use similar styling for elements with the same purpose (e.g., buttons or headings).

Using Anchor Links

Anchor links allow users to navigate directly to specific sections of your site. To set up anchor links:

1. **Assign an ID to a Section:** In the section settings, enter a unique ID (e.g., "services" or "contact").
2. **Link to the ID:** Create a link (e.g., in the navigation menu) and set the target to #ID.

Common Layout Structures

1. Hero Section

- **Elements:** Headline, subheadline, call-to-action button.
- **Container Usage:** Group headline and button for alignment.
- **Styling:** Use a bold background image or color for impact.

2. Services or Features Section

- **Elements:** Icons, text descriptions, and buttons for each feature.
- **Container Usage:** Place each feature in its own container. Use a grid layout for alignment.

3. Portfolio or Gallery Section

- **Elements:** Images or videos with captions.
- **Container Usage:** Group images into rows or grids within containers.

4. Contact Section

- **Elements:** Contact form, email, phone number, and social media links.
- **Container Usage:** Use a container for the form and another for contact details.

Common Mistakes to Avoid

1. **Overloading Sections:** Too much content in one section can overwhelm users.
   - **Solution:** Break content into smaller, focused sections.
2. **Inconsistent Styling:** Mismatched spacing, fonts, or colors can make your site look unprofessional.
   - **Solution:** Apply consistent styles across sections and containers.
3. **Poor Alignment:** Misaligned elements create visual clutter.
   - **Solution:** Use Carrd's alignment tools and grids for precision.
4. **Neglecting Mobile Layouts:** Sections and containers that look great on desktop may break on mobile.
   - **Solution:** Test and adjust your site for mobile responsiveness.

Conclusion

Sections and containers are powerful tools for organizing your content and creating a seamless user experience. By mastering these elements, you can build single-page websites that are both visually appealing and easy to navigate.

Section 4:
Building Your First Single-Page Site

Planning Your Site's Structure

Before diving into the design process, planning your site's structure is a critical step. A well-organized structure ensures your content flows logically, keeps your visitors engaged, and achieves your website's goals. In this chapter, we'll explore how to outline and plan your Carrd website's structure effectively, ensuring a smooth design and user experience.

Why Planning Your Site's Structure Matters

1. **Clarity and Focus**: A clear structure ensures your visitors can find information easily.
2. **User Experience**: Logical content flow keeps visitors engaged and encourages them to take action.
3. **Efficiency**: A solid plan saves time during the design phase by reducing trial and error.
4. **Alignment with Goals**: Proper structure ensures every section serves a purpose, whether it's informing, converting, or engaging.

Steps to Plan Your Site's Structure

1. Define Your Purpose

Start by identifying the primary goal of your website. Ask yourself:

- Is this a personal portfolio to showcase my work?
- Am I creating a landing page to promote a product or service?
- Do I need to capture leads through a form or newsletter sign-up?
- Am I building an informational site to share details about an event or project?

2. Identify Your Target Audience

Understanding your audience helps shape your content and design. Consider:

- Who is your audience? (e.g., potential clients, employers, customers)
- What are their goals or pain points?
- What information are they likely to seek?

3. Outline Your Key Sections

Most single-page websites follow a logical sequence. Below is a common structure you can adapt:

Hero Section (Introduction)

- Purpose: Grab attention immediately with a clear headline, subheadline, and call-to-action (CTA).
- Content: Brief summary of your website's purpose and value.

About Section

- Purpose: Introduce yourself, your brand, or your business.
- Content: Short bio, mission statement, or company overview.

Features/Services Section

- Purpose: Highlight what you offer.
- Content: List of services, features, or benefits with icons or images.

Portfolio/Work Showcase

- Purpose: Provide examples of your work or success stories.
- Content: Image gallery, case studies, or testimonials.

Testimonials/Social Proof

- Purpose: Build credibility and trust.
- Content: Quotes from satisfied clients, customers, or collaborators.

Contact Section

- Purpose: Make it easy for visitors to reach you.
- Content: Contact form, email, phone number, and social media links.

Tools for Mapping Your Structure

Wireframes

Create a basic sketch of your website's layout. You can do this on paper or using tools like:

- Figma
- Adobe XD
- Canva

Content Outlines

Write a list of the sections and the content each will contain. Example:

1. Hero Section: Headline, subheadline, CTA button.
2. About Section: Two-paragraph bio, headshot image.
3. Services Section: Three service descriptions with icons.

Flowcharts

Use tools like Lucidchart or Miro to visualize how users will navigate your site and interact with elements like buttons and links.

Creating a Logical Flow

To ensure your site's structure flows logically, follow these guidelines:

1. Prioritize Content

Put the most important information at the top of the page. For example:

- **Headline and CTA**: First things visitors see.
- **Key Features or Benefits**: Second section to engage interest.

2. Group Related Content

Organize similar information into cohesive sections. For example:

- Combine testimonials, reviews, and case studies into a single "Social Proof" section.

3. Maintain Consistency

Use a consistent layout style for all sections to avoid confusing your visitors.

4. Use Anchor Links

Anchor links allow visitors to navigate directly to specific sections. For example:

- Add "Services," "Portfolio," and "Contact" links in your navigation menu.

Examples of Effective Structures

Personal Portfolio

1. Hero Section: Name, headline, CTA ("View My Work").
2. About Section: Short bio, photo.
3. Portfolio Section: Image gallery or project links.
4. Testimonials Section: Quotes from clients or colleagues.
5. Contact Section: Email and social links.

Landing Page

1. Hero Section: Headline, subheadline, CTA ("Sign Up Now").
2. Features Section: List of benefits with icons.
3. Testimonials Section: User reviews or case studies.
4. Contact Section: Lead capture form.

Event Page

1. Hero Section: Event name, date, and CTA ("Register Now").
2. Details Section: Agenda, speakers, or location map.
3. Testimonials Section: Reviews from past attendees.
4. Contact Section: Email, phone number, and FAQs.

Common Mistakes to Avoid

1. **Overloading with Content**
   - Too much information can overwhelm visitors.
   - **Solution:** Keep sections concise and focused.
2. **Skipping the Planning Stage**
   - Jumping into design without a plan can lead to a disorganized layout.
   - **Solution:** Spend time outlining your structure before starting.
3. **Ignoring User Goals**
   - Failing to address visitor needs can result in low engagement.
   - **Solution:** Align your content and structure with your audience's goals.
4. **Poor Navigation**
   - A lack of clear navigation can frustrate users.
   - **Solution:** Use anchor links and a visible navigation bar.

Conclusion

Planning your site's structure is the foundation of a successful Carrd website. By defining your goals, understanding your audience, and mapping out a logical flow, you set the stage for a design that's both functional and visually appealing.

Adding Text & Basic Elements

Text and basic elements form the foundation of your Carrd website. These elements convey your message, guide visitors through your content, and enhance interactivity. In this chapter, we'll explore how to add and customize text and essential elements in Carrd, helping you create a clear and engaging website.

Why Text & Basic Elements Are Essential

1. **Communication**: Text is the primary medium for delivering information.
2. **Navigation**: Buttons, links, and headings guide users through your site.
3. **Engagement**: Well-placed elements like buttons and images encourage interaction.

Adding Text

Text is a versatile element that can be used for headings, paragraphs, labels, and more.

How to Add Text

1. **Open the Carrd Editor**
   - Navigate to the section where you want to add text.
2. **Click "+" to Add an Element**
   - Choose "Text" from the list of elements.
3. **Enter Your Content**
   - Replace the placeholder text with your own content.
4. **Customize the Style**
   - Adjust font size, weight, color, and alignment in the text settings panel.

Tips for Effective Text Use

- **Headlines:** Use larger, bold fonts for headlines to grab attention.
- **Body Text:** Keep paragraphs concise and legible.
- **Hierarchy:** Use different font sizes and styles to create a clear visual hierarchy.
- **Alignment:** Left-align body text for better readability.

Adding Basic Elements

1. Buttons

Buttons are essential for driving user action, such as clicking a link or submitting a form.

How to Add a Button

1. **Click "+" and Select "Button"**
   - Place the button where you want it.
2. **Customize the Label**
   - Change the button text to reflect its purpose (e.g., "Learn More" or "Sign Up").
3. **Set the Link**
   - Add a URL, anchor link, or email address as the button's target.
4. **Style the Button**

○ Adjust size, color, and hover effects to match your site's design.

Best Practices for Buttons

- Use action-oriented text like "Get Started" or "Download Now."
- Ensure buttons are large enough to click easily, especially on mobile.
- Place buttons prominently, such as below headlines or in the hero section.

---

2. Images

Images enhance the visual appeal of your site and can be used as standalone elements or alongside text.

How to Add an Image

1. **Click "+" and Select "Image"**
   ○ Upload a file or paste a URL.
2. **Adjust Dimensions**
   ○ Resize the image for the desired look and fit.
3. **Add Alt Text**
   ○ Provide a description for accessibility and SEO.

Tips for Using Images

- Use high-quality, optimized images.
- Align images with related text to create context.
- Avoid overloading your site with too many images.

---

3. Links

Links direct users to other sections or external websites.

How to Add a Link

1. **Highlight Text or Add a Button**
   ○ Links can be added to either text or buttons.
2. **Insert the URL**
   ○ Paste the target URL or anchor link.
3. **Customize Link Style**
   ○ Use underline or color changes to indicate the link is clickable.

Best Practices for Links

- Use descriptive text for links (e.g., "Visit Our Portfolio" instead of "Click Here").
- Ensure links open in a new tab if they lead to external sites.

---

4. Dividers

Dividers are horizontal lines that visually separate sections or elements.

How to Add a Divider

1. **Click "+" and Select "Divider"**
   ○ Place the divider where needed.

2. **Customize the Style**
   - ○ Adjust thickness, color, and length to match your design.

When to Use Dividers

- Separate content in a busy section.
- Indicate transitions between different sections.

---

5. Icons (Pro Feature)

Icons are great for adding visual interest or representing features and services.

How to Add an Icon

1. **Click "+" and Select "Icon"**
   - ○ Choose from Carrd's built-in icon library.
2. **Customize the Icon**
   - ○ Adjust size, color, and alignment.
3. **Add a Link (Optional)**
   - ○ Link icons to other sections or external pages.

Common Uses for Icons

- Represent services or features.
- Use as social media links.

Organizing Text & Elements

1. Group Related Elements

- Use containers to group related text and elements (e.g., a heading, paragraph, and button).

2. Maintain Consistent Spacing

- Add padding or margins between elements to avoid clutter.

3. Use Alignment Tools

- Align elements to create a clean, professional look.

Common Mistakes to Avoid

1. **Too Much Text**
   - ○ Overloading your site with text can overwhelm users.
   - ○ **Solution:** Keep content concise and scannable.
2. **Inconsistent Styles**
   - ○ Using different font sizes or colors haphazardly creates visual confusion.
   - ○ **Solution:** Stick to a consistent style guide.
3. **Poor Placement of CTAs**
   - ○ If buttons or links are hard to find, users won't take action.
   - ○ **Solution:** Place CTAs in prominent locations, such as at the end of sections.
4. **Low-Quality Images**

- ○ Blurry or pixelated images reduce your site's credibility.
- ○ **Solution:** Use high-resolution, optimized images.

Conclusion

Adding text and basic elements is the first step in bringing your Carrd website to life. By using these tools effectively, you can create a site that is not only visually appealing but also functional and engaging.

Responsive Design Basics

Responsive design ensures that your Carrd website looks great and functions seamlessly on all devices, including desktops, tablets, and smartphones. With the majority of web traffic coming from mobile devices, designing responsively is no longer optional—it's essential.

In this chapter, we'll cover the principles of responsive design and how to implement them effectively in Carrd.

What Is Responsive Design?

Responsive design refers to the practice of creating websites that adapt dynamically to different screen sizes and resolutions. Instead of designing separate sites for mobile and desktop users, a responsive site adjusts its layout and elements to provide an optimal experience for everyone.

Why Responsive Design Matters

1. **Improved User Experience**: Visitors can navigate your site effortlessly, regardless of their device.
2. **Better SEO**: Search engines like Google prioritize mobile-friendly sites in search rankings.
3. **Increased Engagement**: A responsive site keeps visitors on your page longer, reducing bounce rates.
4. **Future-Proofing**: Ensures your site works on new devices and screen sizes as technology evolves.

Carrd's Built-In Responsive Design Features

Carrd simplifies responsive design with tools and settings that automatically adapt your site to different devices. Here's what Carrd offers:

1. Mobile View Toggle

- Allows you to preview how your site looks on mobile screens.
- Access this by clicking the "Mobile View" button in the editor.

2. Flexible Sections and Elements

- Carrd's sections and containers are designed to adjust automatically to smaller screens.
- Elements like text, buttons, and images resize proportionally.

3. Breakpoints (Pro Feature)

- Breakpoints let you customize specific settings for different screen sizes, offering greater control over your responsive design.

Principles of Responsive Design

1. Prioritize Content

- Place the most important content (e.g., headings, CTAs) at the top of the page.

- Ensure critical information is visible without requiring users to scroll.

2. Use Flexible Layouts

- Avoid fixed widths for sections and containers. Instead, let them expand or shrink based on the screen size.

3. Optimize Text for Readability

- Use scalable font sizes that remain legible on small screens.
- Ensure proper line spacing and avoid overly long paragraphs.

4. Optimize Images

- Use appropriately sized images to avoid slow load times on mobile.
- Enable responsive image settings to ensure images adjust to the screen size.

5. Ensure Touch-Friendly Interactions

- Make buttons large enough to tap easily on touchscreens.
- Add sufficient spacing between clickable elements to prevent accidental clicks.

How to Design Responsively in Carrd

1. Start with a Mobile-First Approach

- Design your site with mobile users in mind, then scale up for larger screens.
- Preview the mobile view frequently during the design process.

2. Use Containers and Sections

- Group elements into containers and sections to maintain a clean, adaptable layout.
- Ensure these elements are set to adjust automatically for smaller screens.

3. Adjust Font Sizes

- Use Carrd's font settings to make text scalable.
- Test different font sizes on mobile and desktop views to ensure readability.

4. Test Button and Link Spacing

- Ensure buttons and links have enough padding and spacing for touch navigation.

5. Optimize Images for Mobile

- Resize large images before uploading them.
- Use image compression tools to reduce file sizes.

Testing Your Responsive Design

1. Preview in the Carrd Editor

- Use the "Mobile View" toggle to check how your site looks on small screens.

2. Test on Real Devices

- Open your site on different devices, including phones, tablets, and desktops, to ensure it works as intended.

3. Use Browser Developer Tools

- Most browsers offer developer tools to simulate different screen sizes.

4. Check Load Times

- Use tools like Google PageSpeed Insights to ensure your site loads quickly on mobile.

Common Mistakes to Avoid

1. **Overloading the Mobile View**
   - Cluttered layouts make navigation difficult on small screens.
   - **Solution**: Simplify content and reduce the number of elements in each section.
2. **Using Fixed Widths**
   - Fixed widths prevent elements from adapting to smaller screens.
   - **Solution**: Use percentage-based widths for sections and containers.
3. **Ignoring Touch Interactions**
   - Buttons or links that are too small can frustrate mobile users.
   - **Solution**: Ensure interactive elements are large and spaced apart.
4. **Not Testing Responsiveness**
   - Failing to test your site on multiple devices can lead to missed issues.
   - **Solution**: Test thoroughly on a variety of screen sizes and resolutions.

Examples of Responsive Design

Responsive Hero Section

- **Desktop**: Full-width background image with large text and a prominent button.
- **Mobile**: Background image cropped to focus on the subject, with text and button resized for readability.

Responsive Grid Layout

- **Desktop**: Three-column grid for features or services.
- **Mobile**: Stacked layout with each feature displayed in a single column.

Conclusion

Responsive design is key to creating a Carrd website that looks and functions beautifully on all devices. By prioritizing mobile users and leveraging Carrd's responsive tools, you can ensure your site provides a seamless experience for every visitor.

Incorporating Backgrounds & Media

Backgrounds and media are essential elements for enhancing the visual appeal and engagement of your Carrd website. They add depth, context, and interactivity, making your site stand out. In this chapter, we'll explore how to effectively incorporate backgrounds and media into your site, ensuring they complement your design and support your content.

Why Use Backgrounds and Media?

1. Visual Appeal

Backgrounds and media make your site more attractive and engaging, helping to capture your audience's attention.

2. Branding and Identity

Custom backgrounds and media elements can reinforce your brand's personality and messaging.

3. Context and Communication

Images, videos, and dynamic backgrounds can quickly convey complex ideas or evoke emotions.

Adding Backgrounds in Carrd

Backgrounds can be applied to individual sections, giving each part of your site a unique look.

Types of Backgrounds

1. Solid Colors

- **Purpose:** Minimalist and clean design.
- **How to Use:**
    1. Open the section settings.
    2. Select "Background" and choose "Color."
    3. Pick a color from the palette or enter a custom hex code.

2. Gradients (Pro Feature)

- **Purpose:** Add subtle depth and visual interest.
- **How to Use:**
    1. In the background settings, choose "Gradient."
    2. Select two or more colors and adjust the angle or direction.

3. Images

- **Purpose:** Create a bold visual impact or set the tone for a section.
- **How to Use:**
    1. In the background settings, choose "Image."
    2. Upload an image or provide a URL.
    3. Adjust settings like size (cover, contain) and position (center, top, bottom).

4. Videos (Pro Feature)

- **Purpose:** Add dynamic and immersive visuals.

- **How to Use:**
  1. Select "Video" in the background settings.
  2. Upload a video file or embed a video URL.
  3. Enable autoplay or loop settings as needed.

Tips for Effective Backgrounds

1. **Prioritize Readability**: Ensure that text over your background is legible by using overlays or contrasting colors.
2. **Optimize for Performance**: Use compressed images and short video clips to avoid slowing down your site.
3. **Keep It Simple**: Avoid overly busy backgrounds that might distract from your content.

Adding Media Elements

Media elements like images, videos, and GIFs can be placed within your site to enhance specific sections.

1. Images

- **Purpose:** Showcase products, portfolios, or concepts.
- **How to Add:**
  1. Click "+" and select "Image."
  2. Upload an image or provide a URL.
  3. Adjust dimensions, alignment, and styling.

Tips for Using Images:

- Use high-quality, optimized images.
- Add alt text for accessibility and SEO.
- Align images with related text for better context.

2. Videos

- **Purpose:** Provide tutorials, demos, or engaging visuals.
- **How to Add:**
  1. Click "+" and select "Video."
  2. Upload a video file or embed one from platforms like YouTube or Vimeo.
  3. Adjust size, alignment, and playback settings.

Tips for Using Videos:

- Keep videos short and relevant.
- Use autoplay and loop sparingly to avoid annoying users.
- Optimize videos for faster load times.

3. GIFs

- **Purpose:** Add fun, animated visuals to grab attention.
- **How to Add:**
  1. Use the "Image" element to upload a GIF.
  2. Adjust dimensions and placement.

Tips for Using GIFs:

- Use sparingly to avoid overwhelming your site.
- Ensure GIFs are relevant and optimized for performance.

Layering Media with Text

Combining text and media can make your content more compelling:

1. **Overlay Text on Images**
   - Add a container with text on top of an image background.
   - Use overlays to improve text readability.
2. **Pair Text and Media**
   - Align images or videos next to text for a balanced layout.
   - Use grids or containers to keep everything organized.

Optimizing Backgrounds and Media for Performance

1. **Compress Files**
   - Use tools like TinyPNG or HandBrake to reduce file sizes.
2. **Use Appropriate Formats**
   - JPEG: Best for photos.
   - PNG: Best for transparent graphics.
   - MP4: Best for videos.
3. **Lazy Load Media** (Pro Feature)
   - Enable lazy loading to delay media loading until it's needed.

Testing Your Design

1. **Preview Your Site**
   - Test how backgrounds and media appear on different devices.
2. **Check Load Times**
   - Use tools like Google PageSpeed Insights to ensure your site loads quickly.
3. **Adjust for Responsiveness**
   - Ensure media elements resize properly on smaller screens.

Common Mistakes to Avoid

1. **Overusing Media**
   - Too many images or videos can slow down your site and overwhelm users.
   - **Solution**: Use media strategically to support your content.
2. **Ignoring Accessibility**
   - Failing to add alt text or captions makes your site less inclusive.
   - **Solution**: Always include descriptive text for images and videos.
3. **Choosing Low-Quality Files**
   - Blurry or pixelated media reduces credibility.
   - **Solution**: Use high-resolution, optimized files.
4. **Clashing Backgrounds**
   - Busy or mismatched backgrounds can distract users.
   - **Solution**: Stick to clean, cohesive designs.

Conclusion

Incorporating backgrounds and media effectively can transform your Carrd website into a visually stunning and engaging experience. By following best practices and optimizing for performance, you can ensure your site remains both attractive and functional.

Saving & Previewing Your Site

Saving and previewing your work are critical steps in the Carrd website design process. These actions help ensure that your site is progressing as intended, free of errors, and optimized for your audience. In this chapter, we'll guide you through the processes of saving and previewing your site effectively, along with some best practices to maintain a smooth workflow.

Why Save and Preview Regularly?

1. **Avoid Data Loss**: Saving ensures you don't lose progress due to accidental browser closures or connectivity issues.
2. **Spot Design Issues**: Previewing lets you identify layout problems, misalignments, or errors before publishing.
3. **Ensure Responsiveness**: Previewing across devices ensures your site looks great on desktops, tablets, and mobile phones.
4. **Boost Confidence**: Reviewing your work step by step builds confidence in the final output.

How to Save Your Site in Carrd

Step 1: Access the Save Function

1. In the Carrd editor, locate the "Save" button in the top-right corner of the screen.

Step 2: Name Your Site

1. When saving for the first time, you'll be prompted to name your site.
2. Choose a descriptive name that reflects the purpose of your project (e.g., "Portfolio Site" or "Landing Page").

Step 3: Select a Save Option

1. **Free Plan**:
   - Sites are saved under a generic Carrd URL (e.g., yoursite.carrd.co).
2. **Pro Plan**:
   - Access advanced save options, such as saving with custom domains or exporting projects.

Step 4: Save Progress Regularly

- After making significant edits, click "Save" to preserve your work.
- You'll see a confirmation message indicating the save was successful.

How to Preview Your Site

Previewing allows you to see how your site will look and function for visitors.

Step 1: Access Preview Mode

1. Click the "Preview" button in the top-right corner of the editor.

Step 2: Navigate Through Your Site

1. Explore the site as if you were a visitor, testing navigation menus, buttons, and links.
2. Ensure all interactive elements are functioning correctly.

Step 3: Check Mobile and Tablet Views

1. Switch to mobile and tablet previews using the device icons in the editor.
2. Verify that the layout adjusts properly for smaller screens.

Step 4: Review Responsiveness

1. Ensure images, text, and buttons resize and align correctly across devices.
2. Pay attention to any overlapping or misaligned elements.

Tips for Effective Saving and Previewing

1. Save Iteratively

- Save your progress regularly, especially after significant changes.
- Use Pro features like versioning (if available) to save different iterations of your site.

2. Preview Frequently

- Preview after adding new sections or elements to catch potential issues early.

3. Test Interactive Features

- Check links, buttons, forms, and embedded media to ensure they work as expected.

4. Use Multiple Devices

- Test your site on actual devices (desktop, tablet, mobile) to confirm responsiveness and usability.

Common Mistakes to Avoid

1. **Forgetting to Save Regularly**
   - Unsaved progress can be lost due to browser crashes or connectivity issues.
   - **Solution**: Develop the habit of saving after every significant change.
2. **Overlooking Mobile Previews**
   - Ignoring how your site looks on smaller screens can lead to a poor mobile experience.
   - **Solution**: Always check mobile and tablet views during previews.
3. **Not Testing Links**
   - Broken links or buttons can frustrate visitors.
   - **Solution**: Test all interactive elements during previews.
4. **Ignoring Load Times**
   - Large media files can slow down your site.
   - **Solution**: Optimize images and videos before uploading.

Advanced Preview Options (Pro Feature)

Carrd's Pro plans unlock additional preview features:

1. **Custom URL Testing**

- Assign a temporary custom URL to test your site's live version before publishing.
2. **Collaborative Review**
   - Share a preview link with collaborators or clients for feedback.
3. **SEO Preview**
   - Use metadata and SEO tools to preview how your site will appear in search engine results.

Final Checklist Before Publishing

1. **Save Your Work**
   - Ensure all changes are saved, and the site name is set.
2. **Preview Across Devices**
   - Confirm the site looks great on desktop, mobile, and tablet views.
3. **Test Interactive Elements**
   - Check all links, buttons, forms, and media.
4. **Review Load Times**
   - Ensure the site loads quickly and efficiently on all devices.
5. **Verify Alignment**
   - Check for consistent spacing, alignment, and overall aesthetics.

Conclusion

Saving and previewing your site are essential steps in creating a polished and functional Carrd website. By incorporating these practices into your workflow, you'll ensure your site is well-prepared for its final launch.

Section 5:
Enhancing User Interaction

Navigation Menus & Anchor Links

Navigation is a crucial part of any website, even on a single-page design. A well-structured navigation menu allows users to jump directly to specific sections, enhancing the overall user experience. Carrd makes it easy to create intuitive navigation menus and anchor links, ensuring visitors can navigate your site effortlessly.

In this chapter, we'll cover how to design and implement navigation menus and anchor links in Carrd, along with best practices for usability and aesthetics.

What Are Navigation Menus and Anchor Links?

Navigation Menus

A navigation menu is a set of links that helps users move through your website. On single-page websites, these links usually point to different sections of the same page.

Anchor Links

Anchor links are links that direct users to a specific section on the page. They use section IDs as targets (e.g., #about).

Adding a Navigation Menu in Carrd

Step 1: Open the Editor

1. Access your Carrd project in the editor.

Step 2: Add a Navigation Element

1. Click "+" in the top-left corner of the editor.
2. Select the "Menu" element.

Step 3: Customize the Menu

1. Add individual links for each section of your site.
2. Set the link type to "Anchor" and specify the corresponding section ID (e.g., #about, #services).
3. Arrange the menu items in the desired order.

Step 4: Style the Menu

1. Adjust the font, color, and size of the menu items to match your design.
2. Choose between horizontal and vertical layouts.
3. Enable hover effects to make the menu more interactive.

Creating Anchor Links

Step 1: Assign IDs to Sections

1. Select a section in your Carrd editor.
2. Open the section settings.
3. Enter a unique ID in the "Section ID" field (e.g., about, services).

Step 2: Link Menu Items to Section IDs

1. In the navigation menu, set each link's target to the corresponding section ID (e.g., #about).
2. Save your changes.

Step 3: Test the Anchor Links

1. Preview your site.
2. Click each menu item to ensure it scrolls to the correct section.

Using Buttons or Text Links as Navigation

If you don't want a traditional menu, you can use buttons or text links for navigation.

Step 1: Add a Button or Text Element

1. Click "+" and select either a "Button" or "Text" element.

Step 2: Link to a Section

1. Set the link type to "Anchor."
2. Specify the target section ID (e.g., #contact).

Step 3: Style the Element

1. Customize the font, color, and size to match your site's design.
2. Add hover effects for interactivity.

Best Practices for Navigation Menus and Anchor Links

1. **Keep It Simple**
   - Limit the number of menu items to essential sections.
   - Use clear, descriptive labels like "About," "Services," or "Contact."
2. **Make It Visible**
   - Place the menu at the top of the page or use a sticky menu that stays visible as users scroll.
3. **Use Smooth Scrolling**
   - Enable smooth scrolling for a seamless transition between sections.
4. **Optimize for Mobile**
   - Use a collapsible or hamburger menu for mobile users.
   - Test the navigation on different devices to ensure usability.
5. **Ensure Contrast**
   - Choose colors that make the menu easily readable against your background.
6. **Highlight the Active Section**

○ Use Carrd's "Active" setting to highlight the current section in the menu.

Advanced Navigation Features (Pro Features)

1. **Sticky Menus**
   ○ Keep your navigation menu visible as users scroll through the page.
2. **Dropdown Menus**
   ○ Add dropdowns for sub-sections or additional links.
3. **Custom Scroll Speed**
   ○ Adjust the speed of smooth scrolling for a better user experience.
4. **External Links**
   ○ Include links to external pages or resources alongside your anchor links.

Testing and Refining Navigation

1. **Test Links**
   ○ Ensure all anchor links direct users to the correct sections.
2. **Check for Responsiveness**
   ○ Test the menu on mobile devices to confirm usability.
3. **Gather Feedback**
   ○ Share your site with friends or colleagues and ask for feedback on navigation ease.
4. **Iterate Based on Insights**
   ○ Refine your navigation based on testing and feedback.

Common Mistakes to Avoid

1. **Using Non-Descriptive Labels**
   ○ Vague labels like "Click Here" confuse users.
   ○ **Solution**: Use clear labels like "Our Services" or "Contact Us."
2. **Overcrowding the Menu**
   ○ Too many menu items can overwhelm visitors.
   ○ **Solution**: Limit your menu to 4–6 items.
3. **Inconsistent Styling**
   ○ Mismatched fonts or colors can make your menu look unpolished.
   ○ **Solution**: Use consistent styling across all menu items.
4. **Broken Links**
   ○ Incorrect section IDs can cause anchor links to fail.
   ○ **Solution**: Double-check all IDs and link targets.

Conclusion

Navigation menus and anchor links are vital for a smooth and user-friendly browsing experience. With Carrd's intuitive tools, you can create a seamless navigation system that enhances usability and keeps visitors engaged.

Creating Contact Forms

Contact forms are a powerful way to connect with your audience, collect inquiries, and generate leads. Carrd provides an intuitive and user-friendly way to add and customize contact forms on your single-page website. In this chapter, we'll explore the steps to create a contact form, customize it to suit your needs, and implement best practices for maximizing user interaction.

Why Use a Contact Form?

1. **Streamlined Communication**: Contact forms provide a simple, direct way for users to get in touch without leaving your site.
2. **Lead Generation**: Forms can capture valuable user information, such as email addresses, for follow-ups or marketing campaigns.
3. **Customization**: Tailored forms allow you to gather specific details, like project requirements or event RSVPs.
4. **Professionalism**: A well-designed form adds credibility to your website.

Adding a Contact Form in Carrd

Step 1: Open the Editor

1. Access your Carrd project in the editor.
2. Navigate to the section where you want to place the contact form.

Step 2: Add a Form Element

1. Click the "+" button in the top-left corner of the editor.
2. Select the "Form" element from the list.

Step 3: Customize the Form Fields

1. Click on the form element to access the settings.
2. Add or edit fields, such as:
   - **Name**: Text field for user names.
   - **Email**: Email field to collect contact details.
   - **Message**: Textarea for user inquiries or comments.

Step 4: Set Up Submission Options

1. Choose how you want to receive form submissions:
   - **Email**: Submissions are sent to your designated email address.
   - **Webhooks (Pro Feature)**: Integrate with third-party tools like Zapier or Google Sheets.
2. Enter the recipient email address or webhook URL.

Step 5: Style the Form

1. Adjust fonts, colors, and spacing to match your site's design.
2. Customize the button text (e.g., "Send Message" or "Submit").

Advanced Form Features (Pro Features)

1. **Custom Validation**
   - Add rules to ensure users enter valid information, such as mandatory fields or email format checks.
2. **File Uploads**
   - Allow users to upload files as part of their submission.
3. **Redirect After Submission**
   - Redirect users to a thank-you page or a custom URL after they submit the form.
4. **Hidden Fields**
   - Include hidden fields to track user details, such as campaign sources.

Tips for Effective Contact Forms

1. Keep It Simple

- Only ask for the information you truly need. A shorter form increases the likelihood of submissions.

2. Use Clear Labels

- Label each field clearly to guide users. For example:
  - **"Your Name"** instead of just **"Name"**
  - **"How Can We Help You?"** instead of **"Message"**

3. Include Placeholder Text

- Add example text inside form fields to show users what to enter (e.g., "Enter your email address").

4. Add a Call-to-Action (CTA)

- Use action-oriented button text, such as **"Get in Touch"** or **"Submit Inquiry."**

5. Ensure Accessibility

- Use sufficient color contrast for text and buttons.
- Label all fields for screen readers.

6. Include a Confirmation Message

- Display a success message after submission to let users know their form was received.

Testing Your Contact Form

1. **Test Submissions**
   - Fill out the form as a user and verify that submissions are received correctly.
2. **Check Email Deliverability**
   - Ensure that email submissions are not flagged as spam.
3. **Verify on Multiple Devices**
   - Test the form on desktop, tablet, and mobile devices for responsiveness and usability.
4. **Test Validation Rules**
   - Try submitting invalid data to confirm that the form's validation rules work correctly.

Common Mistakes to Avoid

1. **Overloading with Fields**
   - Long forms can discourage users from submitting.
   - **Solution**: Limit fields to essential information.
2. **Unclear Submission Process**
   - Users may abandon the form if they're unsure what happens after submission.
   - **Solution**: Add a clear confirmation message or redirect page.
3. **Poor Button Design**
   - A dull or hard-to-read button can reduce interaction.
   - **Solution**: Use a prominent button color and clear CTA text.
4. **Not Testing the Form**
   - Unchecked forms may not work as intended.
   - **Solution**: Test submissions thoroughly before publishing.

Enhancing Contact Forms with Additional Features

1. **Add ReCAPTCHA (Pro Feature)**
   - Prevent spam submissions by adding Google's reCAPTCHA.
2. **Integrate with Email Marketing Tools**
   - Automatically add form submissions to your email marketing list via webhooks or third-party integrations.
3. **Personalize Your Form**
   - Use conditional fields to show or hide questions based on user responses.
4. **Include Social Proof**
   - Add testimonials or trust badges near the form to encourage submissions.

Examples of Contact Form Use Cases

1. Business Inquiries

- Fields: Name, Email, Phone, Message
- CTA: **"Contact Us"**

2. Event Registration

- Fields: Name, Email, Number of Attendees
- CTA: **"Reserve Your Spot"**

3. Feedback Collection

- Fields: Name, Email, Feedback
- CTA: **"Submit Feedback"**

Conclusion

Contact forms are an essential tool for fostering communication and building connections with your audience. Carrd makes it easy to create, customize, and optimize forms to suit your specific needs. By following the best practices outlined in this chapter, you can ensure your forms are functional, user-friendly, and visually appealing.

Embedding Videos & Third-Party Widgets

Videos and third-party widgets are powerful tools for enhancing user interaction and engagement on your Carrd site. Whether you want to showcase a promotional video, embed a map, or integrate external functionalities, Carrd makes it easy to embed and manage these elements. In this chapter, we'll guide you through embedding videos and third-party widgets, along with best practices to ensure they seamlessly fit into your site.

Why Use Videos & Third-Party Widgets?

1. Enhance Engagement

Videos grab attention and convey information quickly, while widgets add interactivity to your site.

2. Expand Functionality

Widgets like calendars, maps, and social media feeds enable features beyond Carrd's native capabilities.

3. Boost User Experience

Integrating dynamic elements like forms, chat widgets, or videos creates a more engaging and professional experience.

Embedding Videos

Carrd supports embedding videos from platforms like YouTube, Vimeo, and others, as well as hosting your own video files.

Step 1: Add a Video Element

1. Click the "+" button in the Carrd editor.
2. Select "Video" from the list of elements.

Step 2: Choose a Video Source

1. **YouTube or Vimeo**: Copy the video URL and paste it into the video settings.
2. **Self-Hosted Video (Pro Feature)**: Upload your video file directly. Carrd supports common formats like MP4.

Step 3: Customize the Video

1. **Dimensions**: Adjust the size and aspect ratio to fit your site's layout.
2. **Autoplay**: Enable this feature to play videos automatically when the page loads. (Use sparingly to avoid annoying users.)
3. **Loop**: Choose whether the video should restart automatically after finishing.
4. **Mute**: Set the video to play without sound by default.

Step 4: Style and Placement

1. Align the video within its section for a balanced layout.
2. Add spacing or padding around the video to avoid crowding other elements.

Embedding Third-Party Widgets

Widgets enable you to integrate tools like Google Maps, Calendly, social media feeds, and more.

Step 1: Obtain the Embed Code

1. Visit the third-party service you want to integrate (e.g., Google Maps, YouTube, Calendly).
2. Generate the embed code from the platform.
   - Example: For Google Maps, click "Share" and select the "Embed Map" option.
   - Example: For Calendly, navigate to "Integrations" and copy the embed code.

Step 2: Add an Embed Element

1. Click the "+" button in the Carrd editor.
2. Select "Embed" from the list of elements.

Step 3: Paste the Embed Code

1. Open the embed settings in Carrd.
2. Paste the embed code into the provided field.

Step 4: Adjust the Widget

1. Resize the widget to fit your design.
2. Use margins and padding to ensure proper spacing.

Popular Widgets to Embed

1. Google Maps

- Add a location map for businesses or events.
- Example: Embed your store location to help customers find you.

2. Calendly or Booking Tools

- Allow users to schedule appointments or meetings directly from your site.

3. Social Media Feeds

- Display live feeds from platforms like Instagram or Twitter to showcase updates or testimonials.

4. Chatbots or Live Chat

- Integrate tools like Drift or Tawk.to for real-time customer support.

5. Analytics and Tracking Widgets

- Embed tracking tools like Google Analytics or Facebook Pixel for performance insights.

Best Practices for Embedding Videos & Widgets

1. Keep It Relevant

- Only add videos and widgets that enhance the content and serve your goals.

2. Optimize for Performance

- Avoid overloading your site with too many widgets or large video files that could slow down load times.

3. Maintain Consistent Styling

- Ensure that embedded elements align visually with your site's design.

4. Test Responsiveness

- Check how videos and widgets appear on different devices to ensure they adapt properly.

5. Avoid Autoplay (When Possible)

- Let users control playback to avoid frustration.

Testing Embedded Elements

1. **Preview Your Site**
   - Use the Carrd preview mode to see how the embedded elements look and function.
2. **Test Interactivity**
   - Click on the embedded elements (e.g., play a video, interact with a widget) to ensure they work correctly.
3. **Check Performance**
   - Monitor page load times to ensure your site remains fast.
4. **View on Multiple Devices**
   - Verify that the embedded elements display correctly on mobile, tablet, and desktop devices.

Common Mistakes to Avoid

1. **Embedding Too Many Elements**
   - Overloading your site can make it slow and cluttered.
   - **Solution**: Prioritize key videos or widgets that add the most value.
2. **Ignoring Mobile Responsiveness**
   - Some embedded elements may not resize properly on smaller screens.
   - **Solution**: Test and adjust dimensions for mobile devices.
3. **Using Distracting Autoplay Videos**
   - Autoplay can annoy visitors, especially with sound.
   - **Solution**: Use autoplay only for muted videos, if at all.
4. **Not Optimizing Video Files**
   - Large video files can slow down your site.
   - **Solution**: Compress videos before uploading them.

Conclusion

Embedding videos and third-party widgets in your Carrd site is a simple yet effective way to elevate user interaction and add valuable functionality. By following the steps and best practices outlined in this chapter, you can integrate these elements seamlessly into your design.

Interactive Buttons & Call-to-Action Elements

Interactive buttons and call-to-action (CTA) elements are crucial components of any website, especially on single-page designs. They guide users toward desired actions, such as signing up for a newsletter, making a purchase, or contacting you for more information. In this chapter, we'll explore how to create effective buttons and CTAs in Carrd, including design tips and best practices to maximize conversions.

Why Are Buttons & CTAs Important?

1. **Direct User Actions**: Buttons and CTAs clearly indicate what you want users to do next.
2. **Boost Engagement**: A well-designed CTA encourages interaction, increasing user engagement.
3. **Drive Conversions**: CTAs are key to achieving your website's goals, whether it's collecting leads or generating sales.

Adding Buttons in Carrd

Step 1: Add a Button Element

1. Open your Carrd editor and navigate to the section where you want to place a button.
2. Click the "+" button in the top-left corner.
3. Select "Button" from the list of elements.

Step 2: Customize the Button Text

1. Click on the button to access its settings.
2. Replace the default text with your desired call-to-action (e.g., "Learn More," "Sign Up," or "Buy Now").

Step 3: Set the Button Link

1. Add a link to the button that directs users to:
   - A specific section on your site (anchor link).
   - An external URL.
   - An email address (e.g., `mailto:example@example.com`).
   - A downloadable file.
2. Test the link to ensure it works correctly.

Styling Buttons

Buttons should stand out visually while remaining consistent with your site's overall design.

Customizing Appearance

1. **Color**: Choose a color that contrasts with your background to make the button pop.
2. **Font**: Use bold, legible text for easy readability.
3. **Size**: Ensure the button is large enough to click or tap, especially on mobile devices.
4. **Shape**: Adjust the button's border radius to create square, rounded, or pill-shaped buttons.

Adding Hover Effects

1. Enable hover effects to add interactivity when users move their cursor over the button.

2. Common effects include color changes, shadow additions, or slight scaling.

Using Call-to-Action Elements Effectively

What Makes a Great CTA?

1. **Clarity**: Use concise, action-oriented language (e.g., "Download Now," "Get Started," "Join Today").
2. **Visibility**: Place CTAs prominently where users can easily find them, such as the hero section or end of a page.
3. **Relevance**: Match the CTA to the user's intent and the section's content.

Examples of Effective CTAs

1. Hero Section CTA

- **Purpose**: Capture attention immediately.
- **Example**: A bold button with "Start Your Free Trial" or "Explore Now."

2. Form Submission CTA

- **Purpose**: Encourage users to complete a form.
- **Example**: "Send Message" or "Subscribe."

3. Purchase CTA

- **Purpose**: Drive sales or bookings.
- **Example**: "Add to Cart" or "Book Your Session."

Advanced Button Features (Pro Features)

1. **Multi-Action Buttons**
   - Add additional functionalities, such as opening a new tab or triggering a script.
2. **Custom Animations**
   - Use animations to draw attention to your CTA, such as pulsing or sliding effects.
3. **Anchor Links with Smooth Scrolling**
   - Create a seamless user experience by linking buttons to specific sections with smooth scrolling enabled.
4. **Dynamic Visibility**
   - Show or hide buttons based on user actions or device types.

Placement of Buttons & CTAs

1. Above the Fold

- Place a CTA in the top section of your site where users will see it immediately.

2. End of Sections

- Conclude each section with a relevant CTA, guiding users to the next step.

3. Sticky Buttons

- Use a sticky button that stays visible as users scroll through your site.

Best Practices for Interactive Buttons & CTAs

1. **Use Action-Oriented Text**
   - Start with verbs like "Get," "Start," "Discover," or "Learn."
2. **Limit Choices**
   - Avoid overwhelming users with too many CTAs. Focus on one primary action per section.
3. **Ensure Accessibility**
   - Use high-contrast colors and large button sizes to make CTAs accessible to all users.
4. **A/B Test CTAs**
   - Experiment with different text, colors, and placements to find what works best.

Testing Your Buttons & CTAs

1. **Verify Links**
   - Test all button links to ensure they lead to the correct destination.
2. **Check Responsiveness**
   - Ensure buttons resize and remain functional on mobile and tablet devices.
3. **Test for Usability**
   - Ask friends or colleagues to navigate your site and provide feedback on CTA visibility and clarity.

Common Mistakes to Avoid

1. **Generic Text**
   - Using vague labels like "Click Here" reduces clarity.
   - **Solution**: Use descriptive, action-oriented text.
2. **Poor Visibility**
   - CTAs that blend into the background can be overlooked.
   - **Solution**: Use contrasting colors and prominent placement.
3. **Overloading the Page**
   - Too many buttons can confuse users.
   - **Solution**: Focus on one clear CTA per section.

Conclusion

Interactive buttons and CTAs are essential for guiding users toward meaningful actions on your site. By designing clear, visually appealing, and strategically placed CTAs, you can boost engagement and achieve your website's goals.

User Engagement Tips & Tricks

User engagement is the lifeblood of a successful website. A site that captivates its audience, encourages interaction, and keeps visitors returning is one that delivers real value. In this chapter, we'll explore actionable tips and tricks to enhance user engagement on your Carrd site. From optimizing design to encouraging interaction, these strategies will help you create a more compelling user experience.

Why Focus on User Engagement?

1. **Increased Time on Site**: Engaged users spend more time exploring your content.
2. **Better Conversions**: Higher engagement leads to more clicks, sign-ups, and purchases.
3. **Stronger Brand Loyalty**: A positive experience encourages visitors to return and recommend your site.
4. **Improved SEO**: Engaged users reduce bounce rates, which search engines reward with better rankings.

Tips for Boosting Engagement

1. Simplify Navigation

- Use a clear and intuitive navigation menu.
- Anchor links and smooth scrolling make it easy for users to explore your content.
- Include a "Back to Top" button for seamless navigation.

2. Create Eye-Catching CTAs

- Use action-oriented text like "Start Your Free Trial" or "Discover More."
- Highlight CTAs with contrasting colors and hover effects.
- Position CTAs strategically, such as at the end of sections or in sticky headers.

3. Add Interactive Elements

- Include hover animations on buttons, images, and links to create dynamic interactions.
- Use forms, quizzes, or polls to encourage user input.
- Embed videos or widgets to provide additional value.

4. Personalize the User Experience

- Use tailored messages, such as "Welcome Back" for returning visitors.
- Add contact forms or chat widgets for real-time communication.
- Offer downloadable resources, like eBooks or templates, in exchange for user details.

5. Optimize for Mobile Users

- Ensure your site is fully responsive and functional on all devices.
- Use large, touch-friendly buttons and avoid clutter.
- Test your site's speed and performance on mobile.

Tricks for Keeping Users Engaged

1. Tell a Story

- Use a narrative structure in your content to guide users through your site.
- For example, begin with a problem, introduce a solution, and end with a call to action.

2. Use Visual Hierarchy

- Place the most important information (e.g., headings, CTAs) at the top of the page.
- Use larger fonts and bold colors for key elements to grab attention.

3. Leverage Social Proof

- Add testimonials, reviews, or case studies to build trust.
- Display the number of users, clients, or downloads to showcase credibility.

4. Incorporate Gamification

- Reward users with badges, points, or progress bars for completing actions.
- For example, use a progress bar on a form to motivate users to finish.

5. Keep Content Fresh

- Regularly update your site with new blog posts, videos, or offers.
- Highlight "What's New" sections to draw attention to recent updates.

Enhancing Engagement with Carrd Features

1. Background Effects

- Use video or parallax backgrounds to create a visually engaging experience.
- Avoid overly distracting effects that detract from the content.

2. Scroll Animations

- Apply fade-in, slide, or bounce animations to elements as users scroll.
- Keep animations subtle to maintain a professional look.

3. Sticky Elements

- Use sticky headers or CTAs that stay visible as users scroll.
- This ensures key actions are always accessible.

4. Forms and Feedback

- Add contact forms or surveys to collect user feedback.
- Use forms as a way to gather leads or offer exclusive content.

Best Practices for Long-Term Engagement

1. **Prioritize Speed**
   - A fast-loading site keeps users from bouncing. Optimize images and minimize animations to improve speed.
2. **Be Consistent**
   - Maintain a consistent design style, tone, and branding throughout your site.
3. **Analyze User Behavior**
   - Use analytics tools (like Google Analytics) to track how users interact with your site.

- Identify areas with high bounce rates and optimize them.

4. **Encourage Sharing**
   - Add social media share buttons to your site.
   - Encourage users to share blog posts, testimonials, or other content.

5. **Provide Value**
   - Offer free tools, resources, or advice that solves a user's problem.
   - The more value you provide, the more likely users are to return.

Common Mistakes to Avoid

1. **Overloading the Site**
   - Too many elements can overwhelm users.
   - **Solution**: Focus on simplicity and prioritize key actions.

2. **Neglecting Mobile Users**
   - A poor mobile experience can drive visitors away.
   - **Solution**: Test and optimize your site for mobile devices.

3. **Ignoring Feedback**
   - Not listening to user input can lead to disengagement.
   - **Solution**: Act on user feedback to improve your site.

4. **Overusing Animations**
   - Excessive animations can slow down your site and frustrate users.
   - **Solution**: Use animations sparingly and purposefully.

Conclusion

Enhancing user engagement on your Carrd site is about creating a seamless, interactive, and valuable experience for your visitors. By implementing the tips and tricks outlined in this chapter, you can keep users interested, drive meaningful interactions, and achieve your site's goals.

Section 6:
Advanced Techniques

Setting Up Custom Domains

A custom domain gives your Carrd site a professional and branded identity. Instead of using a default Carrd subdomain (e.g., yoursite.carrd.co), you can use a unique URL like www.yoursite.com. This chapter will guide you through the process of setting up a custom domain for your Carrd site and explain the benefits, steps, and best practices for seamless integration.

Why Use a Custom Domain?

1. **Professionalism**: A custom domain establishes credibility and trust with your audience.
2. **Brand Identity**: Reinforces your brand by using a memorable, branded URL.
3. **SEO Benefits**: Custom domains are better for search engine rankings compared to subdomains.
4. **Marketing Ease**: A unique URL is easier to share and promotes a cohesive brand image.

Prerequisites

To use a custom domain with Carrd, you'll need:

1. **A Pro Plan**: Only Carrd's Pro plans support custom domains.
2. **A Domain Name**: Purchase a domain from a registrar like Google Domains, GoDaddy, Namecheap, or others.
3. **Access to DNS Settings**: Ensure you can manage the DNS settings of your domain.

Steps to Set Up a Custom Domain

Step 1: Enable the Custom Domain Option in Carrd

1. Open your Carrd site in the editor.
2. Click "Publish" in the top-right corner.
3. Under "Domain," select the "Custom Domain" option.
4. Enter your desired domain name (e.g., www.yoursite.com).

Step 2: Update Your DNS Settings

Once you've set up your domain in Carrd, you need to configure the domain's DNS settings with your registrar:

A Records

1. Log in to your domain registrar's dashboard.
2. Navigate to the DNS or domain management section.
3. Add or update the following A records:

    ◦ Host: @
    ◦ Points to: 192.64.119.38

CNAME Record

1. Add a CNAME record for the www subdomain:
    ◦ Host: www
    ◦ Points to: carrd.co

Propagation Time

- DNS changes can take up to 24 hours to propagate worldwide.

Step 3: Verify Your Domain in Carrd

1. Return to Carrd and click "Publish."
2. Carrd will check your DNS settings.
3. Once verified, your site will be live on your custom domain.

Tips for Choosing a Domain

1. **Keep It Short and Simple**: A shorter domain is easier to remember and type.
2. **Use Keywords**: Include relevant keywords to improve search engine visibility (e.g., yourbranddesigns.com).
3. **Avoid Hyphens and Numbers**: These can confuse users and make the URL harder to share verbally.
4. **Choose a Recognizable TLD**: Popular top-level domains (TLDs) like .com, .net, or .org are often more trusted.

Advanced Custom Domain Settings

1. Redirecting Non-www to www

- Configure your registrar to redirect yoursite.com to www.yoursite.com to avoid confusion.

2. Setting Up SSL (HTTPS)

- Carrd automatically provides SSL (Secure Sockets Layer) certificates for custom domains, ensuring your site is secure and displays a padlock icon in browsers.

3. Subdomain Usage

- You can assign subdomains (e.g., blog.yoursite.com) to different parts of your site or other platforms.

Testing and Troubleshooting

1. **Test Your Site**
    ◦ Visit your domain in a browser to ensure it loads correctly.
2. **Check DNS Propagation**

- Use tools like [DNS Checker] (https://dnschecker.org) to confirm that your DNS changes have propagated globally.
3. **Verify SSL Certificate**
   - Ensure your site loads with `https://` and displays a padlock icon.
4. **Common Errors**
   - **Domain Not Resolving**: Double-check your DNS records for typos or incorrect values.
   - **SSL Not Active**: Wait 24 hours; if the issue persists, recheck your DNS settings.

Benefits of Pro Features for Custom Domains

Carrd's Pro plans offer several additional features to enhance your custom domain setup:

1. **Multiple Domains**: Link multiple domains to a single site or assign different domains to multiple sites.
2. **Redirect Pages**: Use custom domains to create redirect-only sites.
3. **Priority Support**: Get assistance from Carrd's support team for domain-related issues.

Common Mistakes to Avoid

1. **Incorrect DNS Records**
   - Double-check your A and CNAME records for typos or misconfigurations.
2. **Not Testing Before Launch**
   - Always preview and test your site on the custom domain before sharing it with others.
3. **Ignoring HTTPS**
   - Secure your site with SSL to protect user data and boost search engine rankings.
4. **Using an Unrelated Domain**
   - Choose a domain that aligns with your brand or purpose to avoid confusing visitors.

Conclusion

Setting up a custom domain transforms your Carrd site into a professional and branded online presence. By following the steps and best practices in this chapter, you can seamlessly connect your domain and elevate your site's credibility.

Basic SEO & Metadata

Search Engine Optimization (SEO) and metadata are essential components of any website. Even with a single-page design, optimizing your Carrd site for search engines can significantly improve its visibility and ranking. This chapter will guide you through the basics of SEO and how to use metadata effectively in Carrd to drive organic traffic to your site.

What is SEO?

SEO (Search Engine Optimization) is the process of improving your website's visibility on search engines like Google. When your site is optimized, it's more likely to appear at the top of search results, driving more traffic from users looking for related content or services.

Why is SEO Important for Carrd Sites?

1. **Boost Organic Traffic**: Attract more visitors without relying on paid ads.
2. **Improve User Experience**: SEO often involves enhancing the content and structure of your site, making it more user-friendly.
3. **Increase Credibility**: Higher rankings on search engines build trust with users.
4. **Maximize Reach**: Ensure your site is accessible and discoverable by a global audience.

Understanding Metadata

Metadata is the information about your site that search engines and social media platforms use to display your content. Carrd makes it easy to manage metadata for SEO optimization.

Key Metadata Components

1. **Title Tag**
   - Appears as the clickable headline in search results.
   - Example: **"The Carrd Handbook: Single-Page Websites in a Snap"**
   - **Best Practice**: Keep it under 60 characters and include a primary keyword.
2. **Meta Description**
   - A brief summary of your site that appears below the title tag in search results.
   - Example: **"Learn how to create responsive, professional single-page websites using Carrd's no-code platform."**
   - **Best Practice**: Keep it under 160 characters and use actionable language.
3. **Keywords (Optional)**
   - While not as critical as they once were, keywords can still guide content relevance.
4. **Open Graph (OG) Tags**
   - Control how your site appears when shared on social media platforms.
5. **Alt Text for Images**
   - Descriptions of images that help with accessibility and image search rankings.

How to Optimize Metadata in Carrd

Step 1: Access Metadata Settings

1. Open your Carrd project in the editor.
2. Click "Settings" in the top-right corner.
3. Navigate to the "Site" tab and locate the metadata fields.

Step 2: Add a Title Tag

1. Enter a concise, descriptive title that includes a keyword.
2. Example: **"Affordable Web Design | Build Your Single-Page Site with Carrd"**

Step 3: Write a Meta Description

1. Craft a compelling description that summarizes your site's purpose.
2. Example: **"Discover the ease of creating stunning single-page websites with Carrd. No coding required!"**

Step 4: Set Open Graph Tags

1. Add an OG title and description to control how your site appears on social media.
2. Upload an image (e.g., your logo or a featured graphic) for optimal sharing visuals.

Step 5: Optimize Alt Text for Images

1. For each image, click on the element and add a descriptive alt text.
2. Example: **"Responsive single-page website showcasing a modern design."**

Additional SEO Best Practices

1. Use Relevant Keywords

- Identify keywords your audience might use to find your site.
- Naturally incorporate these keywords into your text, headings, and metadata.

2. Structure Your Content with Headings

- Use clear and organized headings (e.g., H1, H2) to structure your site.
- Example: An H1 for your site's title, H2 for section headings, and so on.

3. Optimize for Mobile

- Ensure your site is fully responsive, as mobile-friendliness is a key ranking factor.

4. Improve Load Times

- Compress images and limit the use of heavy elements like large videos or excessive animations.

5. Create Engaging Content

- Write clear, valuable, and engaging content that encourages users to stay on your site longer.

6. Use Internal Links

- Add links within your site to guide users and help search engines crawl your content.

Testing Your SEO

1. **Check Metadata**
   - Use online tools like [Meta Tags] (https://metatags.io) to preview how your metadata appears in search results and on social media.
2. **Test Page Speed**
   - Use Google's [PageSpeed Insights] (https://pagespeed.web.dev/) to analyze and optimize your site's loading speed.
3. **Analyze Mobile-Friendliness**
   - Use Google's [Mobile-Friendly Test] (https://search.google.com/test/mobile-friendly) to ensure your site works well on all devices.
4. **Track Performance**
   - Use analytics tools like Google Analytics or Carrd's Pro integrations to monitor traffic and user behavior.

Common SEO Mistakes to Avoid

1. **Keyword Stuffing**
   - Overusing keywords can lead to penalties.
   - **Solution**: Use keywords naturally and focus on readability.
2. **Neglecting Metadata**
   - Missing or poorly written metadata can reduce your site's visibility.
   - **Solution**: Fill out all metadata fields in Carrd.
3. **Ignoring Mobile Users**
   - A site that isn't mobile-friendly will rank lower in search results.
   - **Solution**: Always test your site's responsiveness.
4. **Slow Loading Speed**
   - Large media files or excessive elements can slow your site down.
   - **Solution**: Optimize all media and streamline your design.

Conclusion

Basic SEO and metadata are critical for making your Carrd site discoverable and user-friendly. By following the strategies outlined in this chapter, you can enhance your site's visibility, attract more visitors, and achieve your online goals.

Tracking & Analytics

Tracking and analytics are essential tools for understanding how visitors interact with your Carrd site. With insights into user behavior, you can make informed decisions to optimize your site, improve user experience, and achieve your goals. This chapter will guide you through setting up tracking tools, interpreting analytics data, and using the insights to enhance your site's performance.

Why Tracking & Analytics Matter

1. **Understand User Behavior**: Learn how visitors navigate your site, what they click on, and where they drop off.
2. **Measure Success**: Track key performance indicators (KPIs) such as page views, conversions, and bounce rates.
3. **Improve Engagement**: Identify areas where users lose interest and optimize for better interaction.
4. **Data-Driven Decisions**: Base your updates and strategies on actual data instead of assumptions.

Setting Up Tracking in Carrd

Carrd supports third-party integrations for tracking and analytics, such as Google Analytics, Facebook Pixel, and more.

Step 1: Choose a Tracking Tool

1. **Google Analytics**: Best for comprehensive site analytics.
2. **Facebook Pixel**: Ideal for tracking user behavior and running ad campaigns.
3. **Other Tools**: Use platforms like Hotjar for heatmaps or Mixpanel for advanced user tracking.

Step 2: Obtain Your Tracking Code

1. Sign in to your analytics platform (e.g., Google Analytics).
2. Create a new property for your Carrd site.
3. Copy the tracking code or pixel ID provided by the platform.

Step 3: Add the Tracking Code to Carrd

1. Open your Carrd site in the editor.
2. Click "Settings" in the top-right corner.
3. Navigate to the "Analytics" section.
4. Paste your tracking code or pixel ID into the designated field.
5. Save and publish your site to activate tracking.

Key Metrics to Monitor

1. Traffic Overview

- **Page Views**: Total number of times your site is viewed.
- **Unique Visitors**: The number of distinct users who visit your site.
- **Sessions**: The total number of visits to your site within a specified time frame.

2. User Engagement

- **Bounce Rate**: The percentage of users who leave your site without interacting.
- **Time on Site**: How long visitors stay on your site.
- **Clicks**: Track where users are clicking most frequently.

3. Conversion Metrics

- **Form Submissions**: Track how many users fill out contact forms or sign up for newsletters.
- **CTA Clicks**: Monitor clicks on key call-to-action buttons.

4. Traffic Sources

- **Direct Traffic**: Visitors who type your URL directly into their browser.
- **Referral Traffic**: Users arriving from other websites.
- **Organic Traffic**: Visitors coming from search engine results.
- **Social Traffic**: Users arriving from social media platforms.

Advanced Tracking Techniques

1. Event Tracking

- Set up specific events, such as button clicks or video plays, to track user interactions.
- Example: Use Google Tag Manager to create event triggers for these actions.

2. Conversion Funnels

- Create a funnel to track the steps users take to complete a goal (e.g., signing up for a newsletter).
- Identify drop-off points to improve the process.

3. Heatmaps

- Use tools like Hotjar or Crazy Egg to visualize where users are clicking and scrolling on your site.
- Adjust your layout or CTAs based on user activity.

Interpreting Analytics Data

1. Identify Trends

- Look for patterns in traffic and user behavior over time.
- Example: A spike in traffic after a social media post or email campaign.

2. Evaluate Engagement

- Analyze metrics like time on site and bounce rate to assess user interest.
- High bounce rates may indicate a need for better content or clearer navigation.

3. Optimize Conversions

- Review conversion metrics to understand how effectively your CTAs are performing.
- Adjust button text, placement, or design to boost clicks.

Best Practices for Using Analytics

1. **Set Clear Goals**

   - Define what you want to achieve, such as increased traffic, higher conversions, or longer site visits.
2. **Monitor Regularly**
   - Check your analytics dashboard frequently to stay updated on performance.
3. **Segment Your Audience**
   - Analyze data by demographics, devices, or traffic sources to tailor your strategies.
4. **A/B Test Changes**
   - Test different versions of your site elements (e.g., CTAs, headlines) to see which performs better.
5. **Act on Insights**
   - Use analytics data to inform updates and improvements to your site.

Troubleshooting Common Issues

1. **Tracking Code Not Working**
   - Double-check that you've correctly copied and pasted the tracking code into Carrd.
2. **No Data Appearing**
   - Ensure you've published your site and allowed time for the analytics tool to process data.
3. **Inconsistent Metrics**
   - Verify that your site is loading correctly across devices and browsers.
4. **High Bounce Rate**
   - Review your content and layout to ensure it's engaging and meets user expectations.

Conclusion

Tracking and analytics empower you to understand and improve your Carrd site's performance. By leveraging the tools and strategies outlined in this chapter, you can make data-driven decisions to enhance user experience, increase engagement, and achieve your goals.

Scroll Effects & Animations

Scroll effects and animations add a dynamic, polished touch to your Carrd site, enhancing user engagement and making your site visually appealing. By animating elements and incorporating smooth scrolling effects, you can guide your visitors' attention and create a memorable browsing experience. In this chapter, we'll explore how to use Carrd's animation features effectively, along with best practices to ensure a professional look.

Why Use Scroll Effects & Animations?

1. **Attract Attention**: Animations highlight key elements like headings, buttons, or images.
2. **Guide the User**: Smooth scroll effects lead visitors through your site in a deliberate, engaging manner.
3. **Enhance Visual Appeal**: Animations give your site a modern, interactive feel.
4. **Improve Content Flow**: Subtle animations help make transitions between sections seamless.

Types of Scroll Effects & Animations in Carrd

1. Scroll Effects

Scroll effects apply movement or changes to elements as the user scrolls through the page.

- **Parallax Scrolling**: Backgrounds move at a slower speed than foreground content for a 3D effect.
- **Sticky Elements**: Certain elements remain fixed in place as the user scrolls.
- **Reveal on Scroll**: Elements appear or fade in as they come into view.

2. Animations

Animations allow elements to move, fade, or transform over time.

- **Fade**: Elements gradually appear or disappear.
- **Slide**: Elements slide into view from a specific direction.
- **Scale**: Elements grow or shrink in size.
- **Rotate**: Elements spin or tilt for added emphasis.

Adding Scroll Effects in Carrd

Step 1: Enable Scroll Effects

1. Open your Carrd site in the editor.
2. Select the element or section you want to apply a scroll effect to.
3. In the element's settings, locate the "Behavior" or "Scroll Effects" option.

Step 2: Choose an Effect

- Select the desired effect from the dropdown menu (e.g., Parallax, Sticky, or Fade).
- Adjust the intensity or duration of the effect, if available.

Step 3: Preview the Effect

- Use the preview mode to see how the scroll effect looks in action.

Adding Animations in Carrd

Step 1: Add an Animation

1. Click on the element you want to animate (e.g., text, button, image).
2. Open the settings panel and locate the "Animation" tab.

Step 2: Select an Animation Type

- Choose from fade, slide, scale, rotate, or custom animations.

Step 3: Adjust Animation Settings

1. **Duration**: Set how long the animation lasts (e.g., 0.5 seconds, 1 second).
2. **Delay**: Add a delay before the animation begins.
3. **Easing**: Choose how the animation accelerates and decelerates (e.g., linear, ease-in-out).

Step 4: Apply Triggers

- Trigger animations based on user actions, such as scrolling, hovering, or clicking.

Best Practices for Scroll Effects & Animations

1. **Keep It Subtle**
   - Overusing animations can overwhelm users. Use them sparingly to maintain a professional look.
2. **Match Your Site's Tone**
   - Choose animations that align with your site's purpose and style. For example, a sleek fade-in might suit a corporate site, while a playful bounce could work for a creative portfolio.
3. **Ensure Responsiveness**
   - Test animations on both desktop and mobile devices to ensure they work seamlessly.
4. **Prioritize Performance**
   - Avoid heavy animations that may slow down your site, especially on mobile devices.
5. **Focus on Usability**
   - Use animations to enhance navigation or emphasize important content, not just for decoration.

Examples of Effective Scroll Effects & Animations

1. Hero Section Animation

- Use a fade-in effect for your headline and a slide-up animation for your call-to-action button.

2. Parallax Backgrounds

- Add a parallax effect to your background images to create depth and visual interest.

3. Section Transitions

- Apply fade or slide animations to elements that introduce new sections.

4. Highlighting Key Elements

- Use a gentle scale or bounce animation on important buttons to draw attention.

5. Hover Effects

- Add animations to buttons or images that activate when users hover over them.

Troubleshooting Scroll Effects & Animations

1. **Animation Not Triggering**
   - Ensure the element's settings are properly configured and the trigger (e.g., scroll or hover) is enabled.
2. **Effects Causing Slowdowns**
   - Reduce the number of animations on the page or simplify their intensity.
3. **Animations Not Displaying on Mobile**
   - Check that the animations are optimized for mobile devices and not disabled in mobile settings.
4. **Confusing or Distracting Animations**
   - Simplify the animation style and ensure it complements the site's design.

Testing and Refining Animations

1. **Preview on Different Devices**
   - Use Carrd's preview tool to test animations on desktop, tablet, and mobile views.
2. **Gather Feedback**
   - Ask users or colleagues to navigate your site and provide feedback on the animations.
3. **Iterate**
   - Refine animations based on user behavior and feedback to ensure they enhance rather than detract from the experience.

Conclusion

Scroll effects and animations are powerful tools to elevate the design and engagement of your Carrd site. By thoughtfully applying these techniques, you can guide your visitors' attention, create a seamless browsing experience, and make your site stand out.

Collaboration & Team Workflows

Collaboration and streamlined workflows are essential when creating a Carrd site with a team. While Carrd is primarily designed for single users, there are several strategies and tools that make it easy to collaborate effectively with others. In this chapter, we'll explore techniques for sharing access, coordinating tasks, and integrating third-party tools to enhance team collaboration.

Why Collaboration is Important

1. **Leverage Diverse Expertise**: Teams can combine design, content, and technical skills.
2. **Improve Efficiency**: Delegating tasks speeds up the site-building process.
3. **Ensure Quality**: Multiple perspectives help identify and address potential issues.
4. **Facilitate Growth**: Team workflows scale as your project or business expands.

Collaboration Options in Carrd

While Carrd doesn't natively support multiple users editing the same site simultaneously, there are several ways to collaborate effectively:

1. Sharing Account Access

- Share login credentials with trusted team members.
- **Best Practice**: Use a password manager (e.g., LastPass) to securely share access.

2. Duplicating Projects

- Use the "Duplicate" option to create copies of a site for team members to work on separately.
- Later, combine the best elements into the final version.

3. Exporting & Importing Sites

- Export a site's JSON file and share it with team members for them to import and edit.
- This is useful for backups or transferring work between accounts.

4. Feedback Through Preview Links

- Share the preview link of your site with team members or clients to gather feedback.
- This allows collaborators to review your progress without accessing your Carrd account.

Using Third-Party Tools for Collaboration

Enhance your team's workflow by integrating these tools:

1. Project Management Tools

- Tools like Trello, Asana, or Monday can help organize tasks and track progress.
- **Example Workflow**: Create cards for design, content, and testing tasks, and assign them to team members.

2. Communication Platforms

- Use Slack or Microsoft Teams for real-time collaboration and discussions.

- Set up dedicated channels for topics like design feedback, content updates, or launch preparation.

3. Cloud Storage Solutions

- Use Google Drive or Dropbox to store and share resources like images, videos, and text content.
- **Example**: Create a shared folder for all site assets to ensure team members have access to the latest versions.

Best Practices for Team Workflows

1. Assign Clear Roles

- Define roles such as designer, content writer, SEO specialist, and tester.
- Avoid overlapping responsibilities to minimize confusion.

2. Set Deadlines

- Use project management tools to set deadlines for each stage of the site-building process.

3. Communicate Regularly

- Schedule weekly or bi-weekly check-ins to review progress and address challenges.

4. Maintain Version Control

- Assign one team member to manage the main version of the site to prevent conflicting changes.

Common Collaboration Challenges & Solutions

Challenge 1: Overlapping Edits

- **Solution**: Coordinate editing times or assign specific sections to each team member.

Challenge 2: Miscommunication

- **Solution**: Use tools like Slack or Asana to centralize communication and updates.

Challenge 3: Inconsistent Design

- **Solution**: Create a shared design system with standardized fonts, colors, and layouts.

Scaling Team Workflows

As your project grows, your team might need to handle larger or multiple Carrd sites. Here's how to scale:

1. Upgrade to Pro Plans

- Pro plans allow you to manage multiple sites within a single account, making collaboration easier.

2. Standardize Processes

- Document workflows for tasks like setting up templates, optimizing SEO, and testing the site.
- Create checklists to ensure consistency across projects.

3. Train Your Team

- Provide team members with resources, such as tutorials or this handbook, to help them master Carrd.

Benefits of Collaborative Workflows

1. **Improved Creativity**: Team collaboration sparks innovative ideas and solutions.
2. **Faster Completion**: Delegating tasks allows simultaneous progress on multiple aspects of the site.
3. **Higher Quality**: Multiple rounds of feedback help refine and perfect the final product.

Conclusion

Collaboration and efficient team workflows are key to creating high-quality Carrd sites, especially for larger projects. By leveraging the strategies and tools outlined in this chapter, you can ensure smooth teamwork, maximize efficiency, and deliver exceptional results.

Section 7:
Publishing & Maintenance

Testing & Finalizing Your Site

Before publishing your Carrd site, it's crucial to thoroughly test and finalize all aspects to ensure a seamless user experience. Testing helps identify and address any errors or inconsistencies, ensuring your site is ready to go live. This chapter provides a step-by-step guide to testing and finalizing your Carrd site, covering everything from functionality checks to mobile optimization.

Why Testing Matters

1. **Enhances User Experience**: Fix issues that could confuse or frustrate visitors.
2. **Builds Credibility**: A polished, error-free site instills confidence in your audience.
3. **Improves Performance**: Addressing technical issues ensures fast load times and smooth navigation.
4. **Ensures Responsiveness**: Verify that your site looks great on all devices and browsers.

Key Areas to Test

1. Content Accuracy

- **Check for Typos**: Proofread all text for spelling and grammatical errors.
- **Verify Information**: Ensure contact details, links, and descriptions are accurate.
- **Consistency**: Maintain uniform formatting for headings, paragraphs, and lists.

2. Functionality

- **Clickable Elements**: Test all buttons, links, and call-to-action elements to confirm they work.
- **Forms**: Submit a test form to ensure submissions are received correctly.
- **Embedded Media**: Check that videos, images, and widgets load and play as expected.

3. Design & Layout

- **Alignment**: Ensure all sections and elements are properly aligned and spaced.
- **Visual Consistency**: Verify that fonts, colors, and styles are consistent across the site.
- **Backgrounds**: Check for proper display of background images and colors.

4. Responsiveness

- **Mobile Devices**: Test your site on various screen sizes, including smartphones and tablets.
- **Desktop Browsers**: Verify compatibility with popular browsers like Chrome, Firefox, Safari, and Edge.
- **Landscape & Portrait Modes**: Check for proper alignment and functionality in both orientations.

5. Performance

- **Page Load Speed**: Use tools like Google PageSpeed Insights to identify and resolve slow-loading elements.
- **Image Optimization**: Confirm that all images are compressed without losing quality.
- **Animations**: Test scroll effects and animations for smooth transitions.

6. SEO Readiness

- **Metadata**: Ensure title tags, meta descriptions, and keywords are accurate and complete.
- **Alt Text**: Verify that all images include descriptive alt text.
- **Page Titles**: Check that each section or anchor link has an appropriate title for easy navigation.

Testing Process

Step 1: Preview Your Site

1. Click "Preview" in the Carrd editor to see your site in action.
2. Navigate through each section to review the design, content, and functionality.

Step 2: Test on Multiple Devices

1. Use real devices or emulators to test your site on desktops, tablets, and smartphones.
2. Adjust elements as needed to ensure responsiveness.

Step 3: Review Browser Compatibility

1. Open your site in multiple browsers to ensure consistent performance.
2. Address any design or functionality issues specific to certain browsers.

Step 4: Conduct User Testing

1. Share the preview link with trusted colleagues or friends for feedback.
2. Ask them to navigate the site and report any issues or suggestions.

Finalizing Your Site

1. Save & Backup

- Use the "Duplicate" option to create a backup copy of your site before making major changes.

2. Address Feedback

- Review feedback from user testing and make necessary adjustments.

3. Set Up Tracking

- Add analytics tools like Google Analytics or Facebook Pixel to monitor site performance after launch.

4. Enable SSL

- Ensure your site uses HTTPS for secure connections. Carrd automatically provides SSL for custom domains.

5. Optimize Load Times

- Minimize large images and animations to improve site speed.

Checklist for Finalizing Your Site

1. **Content**:
   - Proofread text for errors.
   - Verify contact information and links.
   - Check consistency in fonts, colors, and styles.
2. **Design & Layout**:
   - Ensure proper alignment and spacing.
   - Review responsiveness on all devices.
   - Test animations and scroll effects.
3. **Functionality**:
   - Test all buttons and links.
   - Submit a form and verify it works.
   - Check embedded media for playback issues.
4. **Performance**:
   - Optimize images for faster loading.
   - Test site speed using online tools.
5. **SEO**:
   - Add title tags and meta descriptions.
   - Include alt text for all images.

Common Issues & Fixes

1. **Images Not Loading**
   - **Cause**: File size too large or unsupported format.
   - **Solution**: Compress images and use supported formats (e.g., JPEG, PNG).
2. **Slow Loading Speed**
   - **Cause**: Excessive media or unoptimized animations.
   - **Solution**: Minimize heavy elements and use optimized assets.
3. **Broken Links**
   - **Cause**: Incorrect URL or missing page.
   - **Solution**: Double-check all links for accuracy.
4. **Misaligned Elements**
   - **Cause**: Inconsistent spacing or layout settings.
   - **Solution**: Adjust element positioning and test across devices.

Conclusion

Thorough testing and finalization ensure your Carrd site is polished, functional, and ready to provide an excellent user experience. By following the steps and best practices in this chapter, you'll confidently launch a professional single-page website that meets your goals and impresses your audience.

Publishing & Going Live

Publishing your Carrd site is an exciting milestone, as it makes your work accessible to the world. Whether you're launching a personal portfolio, a landing page, or a business website, this chapter will guide you through the process of publishing your site and ensuring a smooth live launch.

Preparing for Publishing

Before you hit the "Publish" button, ensure your site is fully prepared:

1. Complete Testing

- Review all functionality, responsiveness, and design elements (refer to Chapter 31: Testing & Finalizing Your Site).

2. Optimize Performance

- Compress images, streamline animations, and test loading speeds to ensure a fast and smooth user experience.

3. Set Up SEO Metadata

- Add relevant meta titles, descriptions, and keywords to improve your site's visibility on search engines.

Publishing Options in Carrd

Carrd offers several publishing options depending on your needs and subscription plan:

1. Publish with a Carrd Subdomain (Free)

- Example URL: **yoursite.carrd.co**
- This is the default publishing option available on all Carrd accounts, including free plans.

Steps:

1. Click the **"Publish"** button in the Carrd editor.
2. Select the **"Carrd.co"** option.
3. Enter your desired subdomain name (e.g., "mybusiness").
4. Check the availability of the name and confirm.

2. Publish with a Custom Domain (Pro)

- Example URL: www.yoursite.com
- Requires a Pro Standard or Pro Plus subscription.

Steps:

1. Ensure you've registered a custom domain through a provider like Namecheap, Google Domains, or GoDaddy.
2. In the Carrd editor, click the **"Publish"** button.
3. Select the **"Custom Domain"** option.
4. Enter your domain name (e.g., "www.yoursite.com").

5. Update your domain's DNS settings by following Carrd's provided instructions. Typically, this involves:
   - Adding an **A Record** to point to Carrd's IP address.
   - Adding a **CNAME Record** for www subdomains.
6. Save the DNS settings and wait for propagation (this may take a few hours).

Securing Your Site

1. Enable SSL

- SSL (Secure Sockets Layer) ensures secure data transfer between your site and visitors.
- Carrd automatically provides SSL for all published sites, including custom domains.

Steps:

1. After publishing, navigate to the **"Settings"** tab in the Carrd editor.
2. Confirm that SSL is enabled.

Testing Your Live Site

Once published, test your live site to ensure everything functions correctly:

1. Check Accessibility

- Visit your site using the published URL on various devices and browsers.

2. Verify Links

- Test all links, forms, and buttons to confirm they work on the live version.

3. Monitor Loading Speed

- Use tools like Google PageSpeed Insights to test your live site's performance.

Announcing Your Site

Now that your site is live, let the world know!

1. Share on Social Media

- Post your site link on platforms like LinkedIn, Twitter, Facebook, and Instagram.
- Use engaging visuals and captions to attract clicks.

2. Email Your Audience

- Send an email announcement to your mailing list with the link to your site.

3. Update Online Profiles

- Add your site link to your LinkedIn profile, email signature, and other relevant platforms.

Monitoring Performance

After launching your site, monitor its performance to ensure ongoing success:

1. Track Visitors

- Use analytics tools like Google Analytics to monitor traffic, user behavior, and conversions.

2. Gather Feedback

- Encourage visitors to provide feedback via a contact form or email.
- Use their input to make improvements.

3. Regular Updates

- Periodically update your content, optimize performance, and add new features as needed.

Common Publishing Issues & Fixes

1. Domain Not Connecting

- **Cause**: DNS settings not configured correctly.
- **Solution**: Double-check Carrd's DNS instructions and update your domain provider settings.

2. SSL Not Working

- **Cause**: SSL setup delay or incorrect DNS settings.
- **Solution**: Wait for propagation or verify DNS records.

3. Site Not Displaying Correctly

- **Cause**: Cache issues or unsupported browser.
- **Solution**: Clear your browser cache and test on multiple devices.

Conclusion

Publishing your Carrd site is the final step in your journey to creating a functional, responsive, and visually appealing single-page website. By following the steps in this chapter, you'll ensure a smooth and successful launch.

Managing Revisions & Updates

Creating a great Carrd site doesn't end at publishing. Regular revisions and updates are crucial to keeping your site fresh, relevant, and functional. This chapter focuses on best practices for managing revisions, making updates seamlessly, and maintaining your site over time.

Why Regular Updates Matter

1. **Maintain Relevance**: Update content to reflect current information, products, or services.
2. **Enhance User Experience**: Improve usability based on user feedback or analytics insights.
3. **Adapt to Trends**: Incorporate new design trends or features to stay competitive.
4. **Fix Issues**: Address any bugs or outdated elements to ensure smooth functionality.

Tools for Managing Revisions in Carrd

1. Duplicate Before Editing

- Before making changes, duplicate your site to create a backup.
- This allows you to revert to the previous version if needed.

Steps:

1. Open your Carrd editor and click the "Duplicate" option.
2. Save the duplicate under a new name for easy identification.

2. Use the "Undo" Feature

- Carrd includes an **Undo** button to reverse recent edits, making small adjustments easier.

3. Save Incrementally

- Save your progress regularly to avoid losing changes during updates.

Types of Updates

1. Content Updates

- Update text, images, and videos to reflect the latest information.
- Examples: Add new products, update event details, or refresh portfolio items.

2. Design Revisions

- Improve layout, fonts, colors, and overall design based on feedback or trends.
- Ensure changes are consistent with your branding.

3. Functional Improvements

- Add or enhance features like forms, buttons, or navigation menus.
- Examples: Update anchor links, embed new widgets, or improve responsiveness.

4. SEO Enhancements

- Regularly review and update meta titles, descriptions, and keywords for better search visibility.

5. Performance Tweaks

- Optimize images, animations, and other elements to ensure fast loading times.

Best Practices for Managing Updates

1. Plan Updates Strategically

- Schedule updates during low-traffic periods to minimize disruptions.
- Use a content calendar to plan seasonal or promotional changes.

2. Test Before Publishing

- After making changes, thoroughly test your site for responsiveness, functionality, and design consistency.

3. Keep a Change Log

- Document updates to track what changes were made and when.
- This is especially useful for teams managing multiple revisions.

4. Gather User Feedback

- Use analytics tools or surveys to identify areas for improvement based on user behavior.

Responding to Feedback

1. Collecting Feedback

- Share your site with trusted colleagues or users and ask for their input.
- Use tools like Google Forms or embedded feedback forms to gather responses.

2. Prioritizing Changes

- Address high-priority issues, such as broken links or poor responsiveness, first.
- Schedule aesthetic or minor updates for later.

3. Iterating on Improvements

- Continuously refine your site based on feedback and analytics insights.

Common Revision Challenges & Solutions

Challenge 1: Overwriting Important Content

- **Solution**: Always duplicate your site before making significant changes.

Challenge 2: Design Inconsistencies

- **Solution**: Use a shared style guide to maintain consistency in fonts, colors, and layouts.

Challenge 3: Negative User Feedback

- **Solution**: Take constructive criticism positively and make adjustments to address user concerns.

Challenge 4: Performance Declines

- **Solution**: Optimize media files and simplify animations or effects.

Keeping Your Site Dynamic

1. **Add New Features Regularly**
   - Introduce interactive elements like buttons, forms, or videos to keep the site engaging.
2. **Refresh Visuals**
   - Update background images, banners, or icons to align with current trends or campaigns.
3. **Update Content**
   - Post blog updates, new case studies, or recent accomplishments to show growth.

Example Workflow for Managing Updates

1. **Step 1: Plan Changes**
   - Identify what needs to be updated and set priorities.
2. **Step 2: Create a Backup**
   - Duplicate your current site to safeguard against errors.
3. **Step 3: Make Edits**
   - Use the Carrd editor to update content, design, or functionality.
4. **Step 4: Test Thoroughly**
   - Check all devices and browsers to ensure updates are functioning correctly.
5. **Step 5: Publish Changes**
   - Once satisfied, publish the updated site and share the new version.

Conclusion

Revisions and updates are an essential part of maintaining a successful Carrd site. By following the strategies in this chapter, you can ensure your site stays relevant, functional, and engaging for visitors. Regular updates not only enhance the user experience but also help you adapt to evolving trends and needs.

Performance Optimization

A fast-loading and efficient website is crucial for retaining visitors and ensuring a positive user experience. Performance optimization in Carrd involves minimizing loading times, reducing resource usage, and streamlining functionality. In this chapter, you'll learn how to optimize your Carrd site to perform seamlessly across devices and browsers.

Why Performance Optimization Matters

1. **Improves User Experience**: Faster sites keep users engaged and reduce bounce rates.
2. **Boosts SEO**: Search engines prioritize fast-loading sites in search results.
3. **Increases Conversions**: Users are more likely to take action on a site that loads quickly.
4. **Supports Mobile Users**: Optimization ensures smooth performance on slower mobile connections.

Key Areas of Optimization

1. Images & Media

Images and videos often consume the most bandwidth, so optimizing them is essential.

- **Compress Images**: Use tools like TinyPNG or Squoosh to reduce file size without losing quality.
- **Use the Right Format**:
  - Use JPEG for photos and PNG for transparent or detailed graphics.
  - For animations, consider lightweight formats like GIFs or Lottie files.
- **Resize Images**: Ensure your images are appropriately sized for their container to avoid unnecessary scaling.
- **Lazy Loading**: Only load images as they come into view to improve initial load times.

2. Animations & Effects

While animations add visual appeal, overuse can slow down your site.

- **Simplify Animations**: Use subtle transitions and limit the number of simultaneous effects.
- **Optimize Scroll Effects**: Test animations on various devices to ensure smooth performance.
- **Reduce Animation Duration**: Keep animations brief to minimize processing demands.

3. Fonts & Typography

Custom fonts can impact load times, but careful management can mitigate this.

- **Use Web-Safe Fonts**: Stick to commonly supported fonts like Arial, Helvetica, or Times New Roman.
- **Limit Font Variants**: Avoid using too many styles (e.g., bold, italic) of the same font.
- **Preload Fonts**: If using custom fonts, preload them in the site settings to ensure faster rendering.

4. Layout & Design

An overly complex layout can slow down your site's performance.

- **Simplify Layouts**: Use fewer sections and elements to minimize rendering time.
- **Avoid Nested Containers**: Excessive nesting of containers can increase complexity.
- **Minimize Empty Spaces**: Remove unnecessary spacing to improve visual flow and reduce resource usage.

---

5. External Scripts & Embeds

Third-party scripts and widgets can slow down your site if not managed properly.

- **Limit External Embeds**: Use only essential widgets like videos, forms, or social feeds.
- **Optimize Video Embeds**:
  - Use thumbnails instead of autoplaying videos.
  - Host videos externally (e.g., YouTube, Vimeo) instead of uploading large files.
- **Monitor Third-Party Tools**: Periodically check for updates or optimizations from third-party providers.

---

6. Testing & Monitoring

Regularly test your site's performance to identify and address bottlenecks.

- **Performance Testing Tools**:
  - Google PageSpeed Insights: Analyzes speed and provides optimization suggestions.
  - GTmetrix: Offers detailed reports on load time, size, and requests.
  - Pingdom: Tracks performance and uptime over time.
- **Monitor Load Times**: Aim for a load time under 3 seconds.

Best Practices for Performance Optimization

1. Minimize HTTP Requests

- Reduce the number of elements (images, videos, icons) that need to load.
- Use icons or shapes built into Carrd instead of external graphics where possible.

2. Enable Caching

- Leverage browser caching to store assets locally for repeat visitors.
- Carrd automatically supports caching for published sites.

3. Optimize Backgrounds

- Use solid colors or gradients instead of large image backgrounds.
- If using an image, ensure it's compressed and cropped to fit.

4. Test Across Devices

- Check your site's performance on both high-speed desktops and slower mobile networks.

5. Regularly Update Your Site

- Remove outdated or unused elements to keep the site lightweight and efficient.

Common Performance Issues & Fixes

Issue 1: Slow Loading Images

- **Cause**: Large file sizes or excessive image use.
- **Fix**: Compress images and use lazy loading.

Issue 2: Poor Mobile Performance

- **Cause**: Non-responsive design or excessive elements.
- **Fix**: Test and adjust layouts specifically for mobile devices.

Issue 3: Stuttering Animations

- **Cause**: Overlapping or excessive animation effects.
- **Fix**: Simplify animations and test on low-power devices.

Issue 4: Long Load Times

- **Cause**: Excessive external scripts or large video files.
- **Fix**: Limit third-party embeds and optimize media.

Example Optimization Workflow

1. **Step 1**: Run a performance test using Google PageSpeed Insights.
2. **Step 2**: Identify the largest files or bottlenecks in the report.
3. **Step 3**: Compress images and videos, and remove unnecessary animations.
4. **Step 4**: Re-test the site to measure improvements.
5. **Step 5**: Repeat periodically to maintain optimal performance.

Conclusion

Performance optimization ensures your Carrd site delivers a fast and engaging experience for all visitors. By implementing the techniques and best practices outlined in this chapter, you'll enhance user satisfaction, boost SEO rankings, and maximize your site's effectiveness.

Troubleshooting Common Issues

Even with a user-friendly platform like Carrd, you may encounter occasional challenges while designing, publishing, or maintaining your site. This chapter provides solutions to the most common issues Carrd users face, ensuring that you can quickly resolve problems and keep your site running smoothly.

General Troubleshooting Tips

1. Refresh and Test

- Refresh your browser and test your site on different devices and browsers to determine if the issue is widespread or localized.

2. Clear Cache

- Clear your browser's cache to ensure you're viewing the most recent version of your site.

3. Check Internet Connection

- A slow or unstable internet connection can impact the Carrd editor or your site's functionality.

Common Design Issues

1. Misaligned Elements

- **Cause**: Incorrect spacing, alignment settings, or container sizing.
- **Solution**:
  - Use Carrd's alignment tools to position elements properly.
  - Adjust margins and padding to create even spacing.
  - Test on various screen sizes to ensure responsive design.

2. Images Not Displaying Correctly

- **Cause**: Large file sizes or unsupported formats.
- **Solution**:
  - Compress images to reduce file size without sacrificing quality.
  - Ensure images are in a supported format (JPEG, PNG, GIF).
  - Check that the file path is correct for imported images.

3. Text Overlaps or Cuts Off

- **Cause**: Improper font size, line height, or container dimensions.
- **Solution**:
  - Adjust font size and line spacing to fit text within its container.
  - Resize the container to accommodate the content.
  - Use Carrd's "Overflow" setting to prevent text from cutting off.

Common Publishing Issues

1. Site Not Publishing

- **Cause**: Incomplete setup or technical issues.
- **Solution**:
  - Verify your subscription plan supports publishing.
  - Check your internet connection.
  - Save your work and try republishing.

2. Custom Domain Not Working

- **Cause**: Incorrect DNS settings or propagation delays.
- **Solution**:
  - Double-check Carrd's DNS instructions for A and CNAME records.
  - Ensure the domain is active and configured correctly with your registrar.
  - Wait for DNS propagation, which can take up to 24–48 hours.

3. SSL Not Enabled

- **Cause**: SSL setup delay or incorrect domain configuration.
- **Solution**:
  - Ensure your DNS settings are correct.
  - Wait for Carrd to automatically enable SSL for your custom domain.

Common Functionality Issues

1. Buttons or Links Not Working

- **Cause**: Incorrect URL or anchor link setup.
- **Solution**:
  - Check that the URL or anchor link is correctly entered in the button settings.
  - Test the link in preview mode before publishing.

2. Forms Not Submitting

- **Cause**: Missing email setup or incorrect configuration.
- **Solution**:
  - Ensure you've added a valid email address to the form settings.
  - Test the form by sending a sample submission.

3. Embedded Widgets Not Displaying

- **Cause**: Incorrect embed code or unsupported script.
- **Solution**:
  - Verify the embed code is correctly pasted into the widget settings.
  - Ensure the third-party script is compatible with Carrd.

Common Performance Issues

1. Slow Loading Speed

- **Cause**: Large images, excessive animations, or too many elements.
- **Solution**:
  - Optimize images by compressing and resizing them.
  - Simplify animations and limit their use.
  - Minimize the number of elements on your site.

2. Site Not Responsive on Mobile

- **Cause**: Elements not optimized for smaller screens.
- **Solution**:
    - Use Carrd's "Mobile View" to adjust layouts specifically for mobile devices.
    - Reduce font sizes and simplify layouts for better mobile compatibility.

Debugging Techniques

1. Check Carrd's Help Resources

- Access Carrd's official documentation and tutorials for troubleshooting tips.

2. Inspect Browser Console

- Open the browser's developer tools (usually by pressing F12 or right-clicking and selecting "Inspect"). Check the **Console** tab for error messages.

3. Contact Carrd Support

- If you're unable to resolve an issue, reach out to Carrd's support team for assistance. Include:
    - A detailed description of the issue.
    - Steps to reproduce the problem.
    - Screenshots or videos demonstrating the issue.

Preventative Measures

1. **Backup Your Site**
    - Regularly duplicate your site to create backups before making major changes.
2. **Test Before Publishing**
    - Use Carrd's preview mode to identify and fix issues before going live.
3. **Keep It Simple**
    - Avoid overloading your site with unnecessary elements or complex features.
4. **Regular Maintenance**
    - Periodically review and update your site to ensure everything works correctly.

Conclusion

Troubleshooting common issues in Carrd is straightforward with the right approach and tools. By following the solutions provided in this chapter, you can resolve problems efficiently and ensure a seamless experience for your site's visitors.

Section 8:
Special Use Cases & Examples

Landing Pages & Sales Funnels

Landing pages and sales funnels are essential tools for driving conversions, capturing leads, and delivering targeted messages. Carrd's simplicity and versatility make it an excellent platform for creating these types of single-page sites. In this chapter, you'll learn how to design effective landing pages and build sales funnels using Carrd.

What Are Landing Pages and Sales Funnels?

Landing Pages

A landing page is a standalone web page designed to convert visitors into leads or customers. Its primary focus is to highlight a single product, service, or campaign with a clear call to action (CTA).

Sales Funnels

A sales funnel guides users through a step-by-step journey from awareness to purchase. It often involves multiple stages, such as capturing a lead, nurturing them with information, and converting them into a customer.

Key Elements of a High-Converting Landing Page

1. Compelling Headline

- Grab the visitor's attention immediately.
- Clearly state the value proposition of your product or service.

Example: "Unlock Your Full Potential with Our Online Course!"

2. Supporting Subheading

- Provide additional context or details about the offer.

Example: "Learn industry-leading skills in just 30 days with expert guidance."

3. Eye-Catching Visuals

- Use high-quality images or videos that align with your brand and message.
- Show the product in action or highlight its benefits.

4. Call-to-Action (CTA)

- Your CTA should stand out and encourage users to take action.
- Use action-oriented language like "Sign Up Now" or "Get Started Today."

Pro Tip: Place multiple CTAs throughout the page for convenience.

5. Social Proof

- Include testimonials, reviews, or case studies to build trust.

6. Minimal Navigation

- Keep navigation simple or eliminate it altogether to prevent distractions.

Designing a Landing Page in Carrd

1. **Choose a Template**
   - Select a Carrd template designed for marketing or sales.
   - Look for layouts that emphasize a single call to action.
2. **Customize the Header**
   - Add a bold headline and subheading.
   - Include a logo or branding element to establish trust.
3. **Add a Hero Section**
   - Use an impactful background image or video.
   - Overlay text and a CTA button prominently.
4. **Highlight Key Benefits**
   - Use icons or images to showcase the top three to five benefits of your offering.
5. **Incorporate Testimonials**
   - Use Carrd's grid or container elements to create a section for customer quotes or success stories.
6. **Place the CTA Strategically**
   - Add buttons throughout the page that link to a form, checkout, or sign-up page.

Creating a Sales Funnel with Carrd

While Carrd is primarily a single-page platform, it can effectively support simple sales funnels when combined with external tools.

Steps to Build a Sales Funnel

1. **Stage 1: Awareness**
   - Create a landing page that captures interest.
   - Include a form to collect email addresses for further engagement.
2. **Stage 2: Nurturing**
   - Use email marketing tools like Mailchimp or ConvertKit to send follow-up emails.
   - Provide value through free resources, case studies, or exclusive offers.
3. **Stage 3: Conversion**
   - Build a Carrd page with a product showcase and purchase options.
   - Embed a payment gateway like PayPal or Stripe to facilitate transactions.
4. **Stage 4: Retention**
   - Create a thank-you page with additional offers or incentives to keep customers engaged.

Tips for Effective Sales Funnels

- **Simplify Navigation**: Reduce choices to keep users focused on the desired action.
- **Track Progress**: Use tools like Google Analytics or embedded trackers to measure conversion rates.

- **Test & Optimize**: Experiment with different headlines, visuals, and CTAs to improve performance.

Example Use Cases

1. Product Launch

- Use a landing page to build excitement around a new product.
- Include a countdown timer and a sign-up form for early access.

2. Event Registration

- Create a landing page that highlights event details and includes a registration form.

3. Free Resource Download

- Offer a free e-book, guide, or template in exchange for email sign-ups.

4. Service Promotion

- Highlight your service's benefits with a CTA directing visitors to schedule a consultation.

Tools to Enhance Your Landing Page or Sales Funnel

- **Email Capture**: Use Carrd's built-in form functionality or integrate with email tools like Mailchimp.
- **Payment Processing**: Embed Stripe or PayPal for seamless transactions.
- **A/B Testing**: Test variations of your page using Carrd duplicates.
- **Analytics**: Add Google Analytics tracking to measure performance.

Common Mistakes to Avoid

1. **Too Much Text**: Keep your copy concise and focus on key points.
2. **Cluttered Design**: Maintain a clean layout to avoid overwhelming visitors.
3. **Weak CTA**: Ensure your CTA is clear, visible, and actionable.
4. **No Social Proof**: Add testimonials or reviews to build credibility.

Conclusion

Landing pages and sales funnels are powerful tools for achieving specific marketing goals. With Carrd, you can create visually appealing, high-converting pages tailored to your audience. By applying the principles in this chapter, you'll be well-equipped to design effective campaigns that drive results.

Portfolio & Personal Branding Sites

Creating a portfolio or personal branding site is one of the most popular use cases for Carrd. Whether you're a freelancer, designer, artist, or entrepreneur, a well-crafted site can help showcase your work, establish your brand, and attract potential clients or collaborators. Carrd's flexibility and simplicity make it an ideal platform for building a compelling, professional online presence.

Why Use Carrd for Portfolios and Personal Branding?

1. **Simplicity**: Carrd's intuitive interface makes it easy to create stunning portfolios without any coding knowledge.
2. **Customizability**: Personalize templates to reflect your unique style and brand.
3. **Responsive Design**: Your portfolio will look great on any device.
4. **Affordability**: Carrd's cost-effective plans are perfect for individuals and freelancers.

Key Elements of a Successful Portfolio or Branding Site

1. Professional Headshot or Logo

- Include a high-quality headshot or your personal logo to establish a connection with visitors.

2. Clear and Concise About Section

- Highlight your expertise, experience, and what makes you unique.
- Keep it brief but impactful to hold the visitor's attention.

Example:
"I'm Alex, a freelance graphic designer specializing in creating memorable brand identities for startups and small businesses."

3. Showcase of Work or Skills

- Use Carrd's gallery or grid elements to display your best projects, designs, or case studies.
- Highlight a mix of work that showcases your versatility and expertise.

4. Testimonials or Client Logos

- Include reviews or feedback from previous clients to build credibility.
- If applicable, display logos of notable clients or brands you've worked with.

5. Call-to-Action (CTA)

- Encourage visitors to take the next step, such as contacting you, viewing your resume, or downloading your portfolio.

Example CTAs:

- "Hire Me"
- "View My Work"
- "Let's Collaborate"

6. Contact Information or Form

- Add a contact form to make it easy for visitors to reach you.
- Include links to your email, LinkedIn, or social media profiles.

Designing Your Portfolio with Carrd

Step 1: Choose the Right Template

- Select a Carrd template designed for portfolios or personal branding.
- Look for clean, minimalistic designs that emphasize visuals.

Step 2: Customize the Layout

- Use sections to organize your content logically.
- Start with an engaging hero section that includes your name, tagline, and a professional image.

Step 3: Add a Portfolio Section

- Use Carrd's gallery or grid elements to display images, videos, or links to your work.
- Include brief descriptions or captions for each project.

Step 4: Highlight Your Skills and Achievements

- Use icons or bullet points to list your key skills.
- Add a timeline or list of achievements to demonstrate your expertise.

Step 5: Include a Contact Section

- Add a contact form using Carrd's built-in form feature.
- Provide links to your email and social media profiles for additional connection options.

Tips for Effective Branding

1. **Stay Consistent**: Use a consistent color scheme, typography, and design elements throughout your site.
2. **Showcase Your Personality**: Let your unique style shine through in your design and content.
3. **Keep It Simple**: Avoid cluttering your site with unnecessary elements. Focus on showcasing your strengths.
4. **Optimize for Mobile**: Ensure your site looks great and functions smoothly on mobile devices.

Use Cases

1. Freelancer Portfolio

- Showcase your best work to attract new clients.
- Include a CTA to hire you or schedule a consultation.

2. Creative Professional Portfolio

- Highlight your projects in design, photography, writing, or any other creative field.
- Include detailed case studies to explain your process and results.

3. Personal Branding for Job Seekers

- Create a digital resume with links to your portfolio and social media profiles.
- Include testimonials from previous employers or clients.

Enhancing Your Portfolio with Carrd Features

Image Galleries

- Use grid or carousel elements to organize your portfolio visually.

Embed Videos

- Showcase motion graphics, video reels, or tutorials by embedding videos.

Custom Links

- Direct visitors to downloadable resumes, project links, or external profiles like LinkedIn or GitHub.

Form Integration

- Use forms for inquiries or lead capture.

Common Mistakes to Avoid

1. **Overloading with Information**
   - Keep your site concise and highlight only your best work.
2. **Unclear Navigation**
   - Ensure visitors can easily find your portfolio, about section, and contact form.
3. **Lack of Call-to-Action**
   - Include clear CTAs to guide visitors toward the desired action.

Conclusion

A well-designed portfolio or personal branding site can open doors to exciting opportunities and showcase your talents to the world. Carrd provides all the tools you need to create a stunning, professional site with minimal effort.

Event & Registration Pages

Whether you're hosting a webinar, launching a product, or organizing a community event, creating a dedicated event and registration page can significantly boost attendance and streamline the registration process. Carrd's flexibility and user-friendly interface make it a powerful tool for building an engaging and effective event page.

Why Use Carrd for Event & Registration Pages?

1. **Quick Setup**: Carrd allows you to create a professional event page in minutes, perfect for last-minute events.
2. **Cost-Effective**: With affordable plans, you can allocate more of your budget to promoting the event.
3. **Responsive Design**: Your page will look great on mobile devices, ensuring a seamless user experience.
4. **Integrated Forms**: Capture attendee information effortlessly using Carrd's form elements.

Key Elements of an Event Page

1. Event Title and Key Details

- Clearly display the event name, date, time, and location (physical or virtual).
- Use a bold heading and visually distinct section to highlight these details.

Example:
"Tech Trends 2024 Webinar"
Date: March 12, 2024
Time: 10:00 AM PST
Location: Virtual (Zoom)

---

2. Event Description

- Provide a brief yet engaging description of the event.
- Highlight what attendees will gain, such as knowledge, networking opportunities, or exclusive offers.

Example:
"Join us for an in-depth webinar exploring the latest trends in technology and innovation for 2024. Hear from industry leaders and gain insights to stay ahead of the curve."

---

3. Speaker or Guest Lineup

- If applicable, include photos, names, and bios of the speakers or special guests.
- Use grid or section elements in Carrd to organize this information neatly.

Example:

- **Jane Smith, CTO at InnovateTech**
  Expert in AI and machine learning.

- **Mark Johnson, Author of 'The Digital Shift'**
  Leading voice in digital transformation.

---

4. Registration Form

- Add a form to capture attendee details like name, email, and optional preferences.
- Use placeholders to guide users (e.g., "Enter your email").

Pro Tip: Integrate your form with external tools like Zapier or Google Sheets for seamless data collection.

---

5. Call-to-Action (CTA)

- Encourage visitors to register or RSVP with a clear, actionable button.
- Examples:
  - "Register Now"
  - "Reserve Your Spot"
  - "Join the Webinar"

---

6. Countdown Timer

- Add a countdown timer to build anticipation and urgency.
- This is particularly effective for events with limited spots or time-sensitive offers.

---

7. Contact Information or FAQ

- Include a section for frequently asked questions (e.g., "How do I join the event?") or a contact form for inquiries.

Designing Your Event Page in Carrd

Step 1: Choose a Template

- Start with an event-specific template or a blank canvas.
- Ensure the layout focuses on the event's details and call-to-action.

Step 2: Customize the Page

- Use Carrd's section elements to separate content (e.g., event details, speakers, and registration).
- Add background images or graphics related to your event for visual appeal.

Step 3: Add an Embedded Calendar or Link

- Include an "Add to Calendar" button for easy scheduling.
- Link directly to platforms like Google Calendar or iCal.

Step 4: Optimize for Mobile

- Preview your page on mobile to ensure all elements are readable and functional.

Examples of Event Pages

1. Webinar Page

- Use a single-page layout with a banner at the top featuring the event title and date.
- Include a form to collect email addresses for sending webinar links.

2. Product Launch

- Highlight the product with visuals and a detailed description.
- Add a pre-order or RSVP form to gauge interest.

3. In-Person Event

- Include a map or directions to the venue.
- Provide ticket purchase links or QR codes for registration.

Advanced Tips

1. **Embed Video Previews**: Add a short teaser video to excite attendees about the event.
2. **Enable Email Notifications**: Use Carrd's integrations to notify you when someone registers.
3. **Track Performance**: Use Google Analytics or similar tools to monitor page views and registrations.

Common Mistakes to Avoid

1. **Overloading with Text**
   - Keep descriptions concise and focus on key details.
2. **Unclear CTAs**
   - Ensure your registration button is visible and easy to click.
3. **Missing Key Information**
   - Double-check that the event's date, time, and location are accurate and prominently displayed.

Conclusion

Event and registration pages are an essential tool for promoting and organizing events. With Carrd, you can create a polished and professional page that captures attention and drives registrations.

Email Capture & Newsletters

Building an email list is one of the most effective ways to maintain direct communication with your audience and keep them engaged over time. Whether you're promoting a product, sharing updates, or nurturing relationships, Carrd provides powerful tools to create email capture forms and set up newsletters seamlessly.

Why Email Capture Matters

1. **Direct Audience Connection**: Unlike social media, where algorithms control visibility, email allows you to directly reach your audience.
2. **Increased Engagement**: Emails have higher engagement rates compared to other channels like social media ads.
3. **Monetization Opportunities**: With a strong list, you can promote products, services, or exclusive offers.
4. **Data Ownership**: You own your email list, making it a reliable asset regardless of platform changes.

Elements of an Effective Email Capture Page

1. Clear Value Proposition

- Communicate why users should subscribe to your newsletter.
- Highlight benefits like exclusive content, updates, or discounts.

Example:
"Subscribe to receive weekly design tips, Carrd tutorials, and exclusive templates delivered straight to your inbox!"

2. Minimalist Design

- Use a clean and simple layout that emphasizes the signup form.
- Avoid clutter that might distract users from subscribing.

3. Strong Call-to-Action (CTA)

- Use action-oriented text for your signup button, such as:
    - "Join Now"
    - "Get Updates"
    - "Subscribe for Free"

4. Privacy Assurance

- Include a brief statement assuring users that their information is secure and won't be shared.

Example:
"We respect your privacy and will never share your email address."

Setting Up Email Capture in Carrd

Step 1: Add a Form Element

- Drag and drop a form element onto your Carrd page.
- Customize the fields to include at least:
  - Name (optional)
  - Email address

Step 2: Integrate with a Newsletter Platform

Carrd integrates with popular email marketing tools to streamline your email collection process:

Mailchimp

1. Create a Mailchimp account and set up a new audience or list.
2. Copy the Mailchimp form action URL.
3. In Carrd, paste the URL into the "Action" field of your form settings.

ConvertKit

1. Use ConvertKit's form-building tool to create a form.
2. Copy the form's embed URL or code.
3. Add it to Carrd using the Embed or Form element.

Zapier

- Use Zapier to connect your Carrd form with virtually any email platform for advanced automations.

Step 3: Design the Form

- Adjust the font, colors, and spacing to match your site's theme.
- Keep the design consistent to maintain a professional appearance.

Step 4: Test the Signup Process

- Test your form to ensure it successfully captures emails and integrates with your platform.
- Submit a test email and check that it appears in your email marketing tool.

Enhancing Engagement with Newsletters

1. Consistent Communication

- Determine a frequency (e.g., weekly, bi-weekly) and stick to it.
- Provide valuable content that resonates with your audience.

2. Segment Your List

- Use segmentation to send tailored messages based on user interests.
- For example, create segments for designers, entrepreneurs, or event organizers.

---

3. Optimize Subject Lines

- Write attention-grabbing subject lines to boost open rates.

Examples:

- "5 Carrd Design Tricks You Need to Know"
- "Exclusive Template for Your Next Project"

---

4. Include Visuals

- Use images, GIFs, or infographics to make your emails visually appealing.

Advanced Features for Email Capture Pages

1. **Lead Magnets**: Offer a free resource (e.g., eBook, template) as an incentive for subscribing.
2. **Countdown Timers**: Add urgency for time-sensitive offers, like a free guide available for a limited time.
3. **Exit-Intent Popups**: Use tools like ConvertKit to display popups encouraging users to subscribe before they leave the page.

Common Mistakes to Avoid

1. **Overloading the Page**: Stick to the essentials—value proposition, form, and CTA.
2. **Ambiguous Benefits**: Clearly state why subscribing is valuable.
3. **Weak CTAs**: Ensure your CTA is engaging and encourages action.

Conclusion

Email capture and newsletters are powerful tools for audience building and engagement. With Carrd's user-friendly interface and integrations, creating a professional email capture page is simple and effective. Use these strategies to grow your list and maintain meaningful connections with your audience.

Monetizing Single-Page Sites

One of the most appealing aspects of single-page websites is their potential for generating revenue. Carrd's simplicity and flexibility make it an ideal platform for turning creative ideas into profitable ventures. Whether you're selling products, offering services, or generating leads, this chapter will explore various monetization strategies you can implement using Carrd.

Why Monetize a Single-Page Site?

Single-page sites are highly effective for capturing attention and guiding users toward a single goal, such as making a purchase, signing up for a service, or donating. Monetizing these sites is a low-cost, high-impact way to capitalize on digital opportunities, especially for small businesses, freelancers, and creators.

Monetization Strategies

1. Selling Digital Products

Carrd allows you to easily sell downloadable items such as:

- eBooks
- Templates
- Courses
- Stock photos or designs

How to Implement:

- Add a PayPal or Stripe payment button to your site.
- Use platforms like Gumroad or SendOwl for secure file delivery and integrate their links or widgets.

2. Offering Services

Promote services such as consulting, freelancing, or coaching by setting up a compelling site that showcases:

- Service details
- Testimonials
- Portfolio samples

How to Implement:

- Use Carrd's contact form to collect inquiries.
- Embed Calendly or similar scheduling tools for seamless booking.

3. Affiliate Marketing

Single-page sites can be designed to promote affiliate products through content like:

- Product reviews
- Comparisons

- Resource recommendations

How to Implement:

- Use affiliate links from platforms like Amazon Associates or ShareASale.
- Ensure compliance with affiliate disclosure guidelines.

---

4. Lead Generation for Businesses

Businesses can use Carrd to capture leads for products or services by:

- Creating an attractive landing page with a lead capture form.
- Offering free resources (e.g., whitepapers, guides) in exchange for contact information.

How to Implement:

- Connect forms to email marketing tools like Mailchimp or ConvertKit.
- Set up Zapier integrations for automated workflows.

---

5. Memberships and Subscriptions

If you provide exclusive content or ongoing services, consider setting up a membership or subscription model.

How to Implement:

- Link to platforms like Patreon or Buy Me a Coffee.
- Use embed codes or links for user-friendly integration.

---

6. Selling Physical Products

Carrd can serve as a storefront for selling physical products like handmade crafts, apparel, or gadgets.

How to Implement:

- Use payment buttons from Stripe or PayPal.
- Embed third-party widgets like Ecwid or Gumroad for inventory and checkout management.

---

7. Hosting Events or Classes

Promote webinars, workshops, or events by creating a single-page site with:

- Event details
- Registration forms
- Payment options for paid events

How to Implement:

- Use Carrd forms for registrations.
- Embed tools like Eventbrite for ticketing.

---

8. Donations and Crowdfunding

Creators and nonprofits can collect donations to fund projects or causes.

How to Implement:

- Add donation buttons from PayPal or Stripe.
- Embed crowdfunding campaigns from platforms like GoFundMe or Kickstarter.

Design Tips for Monetization Success

1. Focus on a Clear Call-to-Action (CTA)

- Each monetization strategy should revolve around a single CTA.
- Make the CTA prominent and action-oriented (e.g., "Buy Now," "Sign Up," "Donate").

---

2. Use Trust Signals

- Add testimonials, reviews, or logos of companies you've worked with.
- Include secure payment badges to build trust.

---

3. Optimize for Mobile

- Ensure your site looks and functions well on mobile devices, as many users will visit from their phones.

---

4. Keep It Simple

- Avoid clutter and focus on the value you're providing.
- Highlight the benefits of your product or service clearly.

Tools and Integrations

Here are some tools you can integrate with Carrd to streamline monetization:

- **Payment Processing**: Stripe, PayPal
- **E-commerce**: Gumroad, Ecwid, Shopify Lite
- **Email Marketing**: Mailchimp, ConvertKit
- **Scheduling**: Calendly
- **Crowdfunding**: GoFundMe, Kickstarter

Example Scenarios

Digital Artist Selling Templates

- Create a portfolio-style site showcasing your templates.
- Add PayPal buttons for instant purchases.

Consultant Offering Services

- Highlight your expertise and services.
- Include a contact form and a link to schedule consultations.

Affiliate Blogger

- Write a review of your favorite tools.
- Include affiliate links with clear CTAs.

Metrics to Monitor

To ensure your monetization strategy is effective, track the following:

1. **Conversion Rates**: Percentage of visitors who complete the desired action.
2. **Traffic Sources**: Identify where your audience is coming from.
3. **Engagement Rates**: Track how users interact with your site (e.g., clicks on CTAs).

Conclusion

Monetizing your single-page site is both achievable and scalable with Carrd's no-code platform. By implementing these strategies and leveraging Carrd's integrations, you can create a professional, revenue-generating site in no time. Start small, refine your approach based on user feedback, and watch your efforts pay off.

Section 9:
Inspiration & Next Steps

Current Web Design Trends

Web design is an ever-evolving field, and staying informed about current trends is essential for creating compelling, modern websites. Carrd, with its sleek and versatile design capabilities, allows you to embrace these trends with ease. This chapter will explore the most popular web design trends of today and how you can implement them in your Carrd creations.

1. Minimalist Design

What It Is

Minimalism focuses on simplicity and functionality. The trend involves clean layouts, plenty of white space, and the removal of unnecessary elements.

Why It's Popular

- Reduces cognitive load for users.
- Directs focus to essential content and actions.
- Improves load times, especially on mobile devices.

How to Apply in Carrd

- Use simple, clean templates.
- Limit the number of colors, fonts, and design elements.
- Rely on spacing and alignment to create visual balance.

2. Bold Typography

What It Is

Typography becomes a central design feature, using bold, oversized fonts to capture attention.

Why It's Popular

- Adds personality and character to a site.
- Communicates brand identity effectively.
- Creates a visual hierarchy.

How to Apply in Carrd

- Choose bold fonts for headlines.
- Experiment with contrast between font sizes.
- Use Carrd's typography settings to adjust weight, spacing, and alignment.

3. Dark Mode

What It Is

A color scheme where light text appears on dark backgrounds, offering a sleek and modern aesthetic.

Why It's Popular

- Reduces eye strain, especially in low-light environments.
- Gives websites a futuristic and high-tech feel.
- Conserves battery life on OLED screens.

How to Apply in Carrd

- Select dark-themed templates.
- Use muted colors and avoid overly bright accents.
- Ensure text and elements have sufficient contrast for readability.

---

4. Micro-Interactions

What It Is

Small, interactive animations that respond to user actions, such as hovering, clicking, or scrolling.

Why It's Popular

- Enhances user engagement.
- Provides instant feedback to user actions.
- Adds a layer of delight to the user experience.

How to Apply in Carrd

- Use scroll animations or hover effects.
- Incorporate subtle movements in buttons or anchor links.
- Test animations to ensure they're smooth and not overwhelming.

---

5. Asymmetrical Layouts

What It Is

Layouts that break away from traditional grid systems, creating a more dynamic and visually interesting design.

Why It's Popular

- Feels modern and innovative.
- Draws attention to specific elements.
- Encourages exploration of the content.

How to Apply in Carrd

- Use custom positioning for sections and containers.
- Play with overlapping elements and staggered layouts.
- Balance asymmetry with readability and usability.

6. Gradients and Abstract Shapes

What It Is

The use of gradients for backgrounds and abstract, fluid shapes to add visual depth and interest.

Why It's Popular

- Offers a modern, artistic vibe.
- Breaks the monotony of flat designs.
- Encourages creativity and experimentation.

How to Apply in Carrd

- Use gradient overlays in background settings.
- Incorporate SVG files or custom graphics for abstract shapes.
- Pair gradients with bold typography or minimal layouts.

7. Accessibility-Focused Design

What It Is

Designing websites with accessibility in mind, ensuring they are usable for all individuals, including those with disabilities.

Why It's Popular

- Expands the potential audience for your site.
- Enhances usability and user satisfaction.
- Aligns with global web accessibility standards (e.g., WCAG).

How to Apply in Carrd

- Use high-contrast text and background combinations.
- Add alt text to images for screen readers.
- Test navigation using a keyboard-only setup.

8. Video Backgrounds and Visual Storytelling

What It Is

Incorporating video elements into website backgrounds or using them to tell a brand story.

Why It's Popular

- Grabs attention and keeps users engaged.
- Communicates complex ideas quickly.
- Adds a premium, professional feel.

How to Apply in Carrd

- Use video embeds or Carrd's background video option.
- Ensure videos are optimized for fast loading.

- Pair videos with concise, impactful text.

---

9. Personalization and Interactivity

What It Is

Creating tailored experiences that feel unique to each visitor, such as customized content or interactive elements.

Why It's Popular

- Increases user engagement and retention.
- Makes the site feel more relevant and useful.
- Encourages repeat visits.

How to Apply in Carrd

- Add dynamic forms or quizzes using third-party embeds.
- Use interactive buttons that reveal hidden content.
- Incorporate tools like Typeform for advanced personalization.

---

10. Sustainability in Web Design

What It Is

Creating websites that prioritize sustainability by optimizing performance and reducing energy consumption.

Why It's Popular

- Aligns with global environmental concerns.
- Improves site performance and load times.
- Demonstrates brand responsibility.

How to Apply in Carrd

- Compress images to reduce file sizes.
- Use minimal animations to lower CPU usage.
- Optimize for mobile-first design.

Staying Ahead of Trends

While these trends are popular today, web design continues to evolve. Regularly explore design blogs, online portfolios, and Carrd's template library for inspiration. Remember, trends should enhance the user experience and align with your website's purpose—choose the ones that best fit your goals.

Beyond Carrd—Integrations & Extensions

While Carrd is a powerful platform on its own, its potential truly expands when combined with external integrations and extensions. These tools enable you to add advanced functionality to your single-page website, turning it into a dynamic, multi-functional platform. This chapter will explore popular integrations and extensions you can use with Carrd and guide you on how to implement them effectively.

1. Email Marketing Integrations

Why Use Email Marketing?

Building an email list is crucial for engaging with your audience, promoting products or services, and nurturing customer relationships. Carrd makes it simple to collect email addresses through forms.

Popular Tools

- **Mailchimp**: Automate email campaigns and manage subscriber lists.
- **ConvertKit**: Perfect for creators looking to build and nurture an audience.
- **MailerLite**: A user-friendly option with advanced automation features.

How to Integrate

- Use Carrd's native form builder to collect email addresses.
- Connect your form to an email marketing tool using API keys or third-party connectors like Zapier.

2. E-Commerce Platforms

Why Add E-Commerce?

Whether you're selling digital downloads, physical products, or services, integrating an e-commerce solution can turn your Carrd site into a profitable storefront.

Popular Tools

- **PayPal**: Simplify payment processing with secure buttons or embedded forms.
- **Gumroad**: Sell digital products and memberships seamlessly.
- **Stripe**: Enable credit card payments with a professional checkout experience.

How to Integrate

- Add payment buttons or embed payment widgets directly from your chosen platform.
- For digital downloads, use platforms like Gumroad to handle file delivery automatically.

3. Scheduling and Appointments

Why Use Scheduling Tools?

For businesses like consultants, fitness trainers, or service providers, offering online scheduling can improve client convenience and streamline bookings.

Popular Tools

- **Calendly**: Allows clients to book appointments based on your availability.
- **Acuity Scheduling**: Provides customizable scheduling options and payment integrations.
- **Setmore**: Ideal for small businesses with multiple team members.

How to Integrate

- Embed your scheduling tool's widget or link directly to your booking page.
- Customize your scheduling options to match your brand's aesthetics.

---

4. Analytics and Tracking

Why Use Analytics?

Understanding your audience's behavior is critical for optimizing your site's performance and achieving your goals.

Popular Tools

- **Google Analytics**: Track user interactions, traffic sources, and conversions.
- **Hotjar**: Gain insights through heatmaps and visitor recordings.
- **Fathom Analytics**: A privacy-focused alternative to Google Analytics.

How to Integrate

- Add the tracking code provided by your analytics tool in Carrd's **Settings** > **Analytics** section.
- Monitor your dashboard for actionable insights.

---

5. Chat and Support Tools

Why Add Chat Features?

Offering real-time communication options can enhance customer satisfaction and resolve queries promptly.

Popular Tools

- **Tawk.to**: A free live chat tool with rich features.
- **Drift**: Combines live chat with marketing automation.
- **Intercom**: Offers advanced customer support and engagement solutions.

How to Integrate

- Embed the chat widget script in Carrd's **Code** section.
- Customize the widget to match your brand colors and tone.

---

6. Social Media Feeds and Sharing

Why Use Social Media Tools?

Promote your content, increase engagement, and drive traffic to your social profiles by embedding social media feeds or sharing buttons.

Popular Tools

- **EmbedSocial**: Display Instagram, Facebook, or Twitter feeds.
- **AddThis**: Add social sharing buttons to your site.
- **Flockler**: Create a social media wall for real-time updates.

How to Integrate

- Embed the widget code for your social media tool in the desired section of your Carrd site.
- Use sharing buttons to encourage visitors to spread the word about your site.

---

7. Workflow Automation

Why Use Automation?

Simplify repetitive tasks by connecting Carrd to other tools in your workflow.

Popular Tools

- **Zapier**: Connect Carrd to thousands of apps, such as Google Sheets, Slack, or Dropbox.
- **Make (formerly Integromat)**: Automate complex workflows with visual drag-and-drop tools.

How to Integrate

- Set up a trigger-action workflow using Zapier or Make.
- Test the automation to ensure smooth operation.

---

8. Advanced Customization with Code

Why Use Custom Code?

For users with coding knowledge, custom scripts can unlock features and designs beyond Carrd's native capabilities.

Popular Tools

- **CodePen**: Test and integrate custom HTML, CSS, or JavaScript snippets.
- **GitHub**: Host and manage custom code repositories for your Carrd projects.

How to Integrate

- Use Carrd's **Embed** or **Code** elements to add your custom code.
- Preview and test your site to ensure the code works as intended.

---

9. Embedding Forms and Surveys

Why Use Forms and Surveys?

Gather valuable feedback, conduct surveys, or create quizzes to engage with your audience.

Popular Tools

- **Typeform**: Design conversational forms and surveys.
- **Google Forms**: Create simple, shareable forms.
- **SurveyMonkey**: Conduct in-depth surveys for detailed analytics.

How to Integrate

- Embed the form link or iframe code directly in Carrd.
- Customize the design to align with your site's aesthetic.

---

10. SEO and Performance Optimization Tools

Why Optimize?

Boost your site's visibility on search engines and ensure fast load times for a seamless user experience.

Popular Tools

- **Yoast SEO**: Generate SEO-friendly meta descriptions and keywords.
- **Pingdom**: Test your site's load speed and identify bottlenecks.
- **TinyPNG**: Optimize images for faster loading.

How to Integrate

- Add SEO keywords and metadata in Carrd's **Settings**.
- Optimize images before uploading them to Carrd.

Unlocking Carrd's Full Potential

Integrating third-party tools and extensions elevates your Carrd website from a simple single-page site to a robust, interactive platform tailored to your needs. Start small with the integrations that align with your goals and audience, and expand as your requirements grow.

Comparing Carrd with Other No-Code Platforms

Carrd has established itself as a favorite among creators and businesses for building quick, visually appealing single-page websites. However, the no-code space is vast, with several platforms offering unique features tailored to different needs. In this chapter, we'll compare Carrd with some of the most popular no-code platforms, highlighting their strengths, weaknesses, and ideal use cases.

1. Carrd vs. Wix

Overview of Wix

Wix is a well-known website builder with extensive tools for creating multi-page and single-page websites. It offers a drag-and-drop editor, advanced design features, and app integrations.

Comparison

Feature	Carrd	Wix
Ease of Use	Intuitive and beginner-friendly	Drag-and-drop but slightly steeper learning curve
Focus	Single-page websites	Multi-page and single-page websites
Design Options	Clean, minimalistic templates	More variety but can feel overwhelming
Pricing	Affordable and transparent	Higher pricing for premium features
Ideal Use Case	Landing pages, portfolios, simple sites	Full-scale business websites

Verdict: Carrd is better for quick, cost-effective single-page sites, while Wix is more suitable for complex, multi-page projects.

2. Carrd vs. Squarespace

Overview of Squarespace

Squarespace is renowned for its sleek, professional templates and focus on creatives like photographers, designers, and small business owners.

Comparison

Feature	Carrd	Squarespace
Templates	Lightweight, fast-loading templates	High-quality, artistic templates
Customization	Limited but straightforward	More customization options
SEO Tools	Basic SEO functionality	Advanced SEO capabilities

| E-Commerce | Limited (via third-party integrations) | Built-in e-commerce features |
| Ideal Use Case | Simple designs for small projects | Portfolios, creative businesses, and online stores |

Verdict: Choose Carrd for quick, minimalist sites and Squarespace for design-heavy, content-rich websites.

---

3. Carrd vs. Webflow

Overview of Webflow

Webflow is a platform designed for designers and developers who want more control over their sites. It bridges the gap between no-code and custom coding.

Comparison

Feature	Carrd	Webflow
Complexity	Beginner-friendly	Advanced; suited for professionals
Design Flexibility	Limited to simple layouts	Pixel-perfect control over designs
Learning Curve	Minimal	Steeper; requires time to master
Use Cases	Simple pages with minimal interactivity	Complex, interactive websites

Verdict: Carrd is ideal for users with no technical background, while Webflow caters to those needing advanced design and interaction capabilities.

---

4. Carrd vs. WordPress

Overview of WordPress

WordPress is the most widely used content management system (CMS), offering extensive customization options through plugins, themes, and coding.

Comparison

Feature	Carrd	WordPress
Simplicity	Extremely simple	Requires maintenance and setup
Plugins	Limited (via embeds and integrations)	Thousands of plugins for functionality
Hosting	Hosted by Carrd	Requires separate hosting
Cost	Transparent pricing	Varies depending on hosting and plugins

Verdict: Carrd is perfect for lightweight, low-maintenance websites, whereas WordPress is better for scalable, content-rich websites.

---

5. Carrd vs. Shopify

Overview of Shopify

Shopify specializes in building e-commerce websites with a focus on online selling and product management.

Comparison

Feature	Carrd	Shopify
E-Commerce Focus	Limited; relies on third-party tools	Full e-commerce suite
Ease of Use	Simple setup for non-commerce sites	User-friendly but focused on online stores
Payment Integration	Basic integration through PayPal or Stripe	Advanced options, including POS
Scalability	Better for small-scale projects	Scales well with business growth

Verdict: Carrd is great for single-product or service pages, but Shopify excels at managing large online stores.

---

6. Carrd vs. Other No-Code Tools

Platform	Strengths	Weaknesses
Bubble	Build complex web apps with no code	Steep learning curve; overkill for simple sites
Tilda	Beautifully designed landing pages	Limited features for interactive elements
Notion (as a website)	Great for personal knowledge bases or portfolios	Limited design flexibility

---

Choosing the Right Platform

When comparing Carrd to other platforms, the choice ultimately depends on your specific needs:

- **Choose Carrd if:** You need a fast, affordable, and easy-to-use platform for single-page websites.
- **Choose alternatives if:** You require multi-page functionality, advanced customization, or specialized features like e-commerce or app development.

By understanding Carrd's strengths and limitations, you can leverage its simplicity and efficiency while exploring complementary tools when needed.

Future of No-Code Design

The no-code revolution has significantly transformed the web development landscape, making it accessible to creators, entrepreneurs, and professionals without a technical background. Tools like Carrd have paved the way for this shift, empowering users to bring their ideas to life quickly and affordably. However, the no-code movement is still evolving, and its future holds exciting potential. In this chapter, we'll explore key trends, advancements, and the implications of no-code design for the years ahead.

1. Greater Accessibility and Adoption

Bridging the Digital Divide

No-code platforms will continue to democratize access to digital creation. By reducing technical barriers, more individuals from diverse industries and backgrounds can leverage these tools to build websites, apps, and other digital products. This shift will likely result in:

- Increased small business adoption.
- Broader use in developing countries where access to technical resources is limited.
- Expansion of no-code tools into education, enabling students to build digital solutions early in their careers.

Integration with Everyday Tools

As the no-code ecosystem grows, seamless integration with other commonly used tools (like Google Workspace, Airtable, and Zapier) will make these platforms even more accessible. This will reduce the learning curve and allow users to automate workflows effortlessly.

2. AI-Powered Design and Development

Smart Design Suggestions

Artificial intelligence will play a pivotal role in advancing no-code platforms. Imagine tools that:

- Suggest optimal layouts, color schemes, and content arrangements based on your brand identity.
- Automatically analyze user engagement data to recommend improvements for your site.

Automated Customization

AI could bridge the gap between pre-built templates and full customization by dynamically adapting designs to specific industries, target audiences, or trends, ensuring that every website feels unique and tailored.

3. Advanced Features for Non-Coders

Scalable Solutions

As no-code platforms mature, they'll incorporate more advanced functionalities traditionally reserved for developers. Expect features such as:

- Built-in database management.
- Complex e-commerce capabilities.

- Advanced API integrations.

Interactive and Dynamic Content

Future no-code tools may allow for the creation of highly interactive and dynamic web applications, including:

- Real-time updates without the need for coding.
- Integration of augmented reality (AR) or virtual reality (VR) experiences for industries like retail, education, and entertainment.

---

4. Cross-Platform and Device Optimization

Universal Design Standards

No-code platforms will prioritize tools that ensure seamless design across all devices, from mobile phones to desktops and even wearable tech.

Progressive Web Applications (PWAs)

The line between websites and apps is blurring. Expect no-code platforms to increasingly support the creation of PWAs, which function like apps but run within a browser, offering features like offline usage and push notifications.

---

5. Personalization Through Data

Dynamic Content Delivery

With advancements in data integration, no-code platforms will allow for:

- Personalizing user experiences based on real-time data, such as location, behavior, or preferences.
- Building marketing campaigns directly within platforms like Carrd to target audiences effectively.

Built-in Analytics

Enhanced analytics tools will become standard, enabling users to measure performance, track user engagement, and refine their designs without needing third-party services.

---

6. Expansion Beyond Websites

Beyond Single-Page Sites

While platforms like Carrd are optimized for single-page websites, the future may see no-code tools branching into:

- Multi-page sites with interconnected layouts.
- Full-fledged web applications or software tools.

Integration with IoT and Emerging Tech

No-code platforms may enable users to design dashboards and interfaces for IoT (Internet of Things) devices, expanding their use cases to smart homes, healthcare devices, and beyond.

7. Ethical Considerations in No-Code

Data Privacy and Security

As no-code platforms become more powerful, ensuring robust security and compliance with global data privacy laws will be essential. Users will demand:

- End-to-end encryption for their data and their customers' information.
- Transparent data usage policies.

Design Ethics

No-code creators will need guidance to build inclusive, user-friendly designs that prioritize accessibility for all users, including those with disabilities.

8. Community and Collaboration

Global No-Code Communities

The no-code movement is fueled by its vibrant community. Expect to see:

- More collaborative tools within platforms, allowing teams to build and iterate together.
- Global networks of no-code enthusiasts sharing templates, tips, and use cases.

Marketplace Ecosystems

Platforms may develop marketplaces for templates, plugins, and integrations, allowing creators to monetize their designs while expanding the functionality of no-code tools.

Final Thoughts

The future of no-code design is bright, with tools like Carrd at the forefront of a transformative era. As technology advances, the possibilities for creators will expand, making it easier than ever to turn ideas into reality. Whether you're an entrepreneur, educator, artist, or hobbyist, the no-code revolution ensures that you can build digital solutions that are functional, beautiful, and impactful.

Appendices

Appendix A: Glossary of Key Carrd & Web Design Terms

This glossary serves as a quick reference to key terms and concepts used throughout this book and within the Carrd platform. Familiarity with these terms will enhance your understanding and efficiency as you build your single-page website.

A

Anchor Link
A link that directs users to a specific section of the same page, improving navigation on single-page websites.

Aspect Ratio
The proportional relationship between an element's width and height, commonly used when working with images and videos.

Animation
Visual effects applied to elements to create movement, such as fades, slides, or bounces, enhancing user engagement.

B

Background Overlay
A semi-transparent layer placed over a background image or color to improve readability of text elements.

Breakpoints
Specific screen sizes where a website's layout adapts to ensure optimal display across devices (e.g., mobile, tablet, desktop).

C

Call-to-Action (CTA)
A button, link, or element designed to prompt users to take a specific action, such as "Sign Up" or "Learn More."

Container
A design element in Carrd used to group and organize content elements, such as text, images, or buttons, within a defined area.

Custom Domain
A unique, personalized website address (e.g., www.yourname.com) that can be connected to your Carrd project.

D

Dashboard
The main interface in Carrd where you manage projects, templates, and account settings.

Drag-and-Drop Interface
A user-friendly design feature allowing elements to be repositioned or resized by clicking and dragging.

E

Element
Any individual component added to your Carrd site, such as text, images, videos, buttons, or forms.

Embedded Widget
A third-party tool or feature, such as a YouTube video or Twitter feed, integrated directly into your Carrd page.

F

Flat Design
A minimalist design style that focuses on simple, two-dimensional elements without excessive gradients or textures.

Flexbox
A layout model in web design that helps in arranging elements efficiently, even when screen sizes vary.

G

Grid Layout
A design framework using rows and columns to structure and align elements consistently across the page.

H

Hero Section
The prominent, visually impactful area at the top of a webpage, often containing a headline, subheadline, and call-to-action.

Hover Effect
An interactive design feature triggered when a user hovers their cursor over an element, such as a button changing color.

I

Interaction Design
The practice of creating engaging interfaces with well-thought-out responses to user actions, such as clicks or scrolls.

Iterative Design
A process of continuous testing and refinement to improve your website's functionality and user experience.

L

Landing Page
A standalone webpage focused on a single objective, such as capturing leads or promoting a product.

Lazy Loading
A technique where images and media load only when they enter the user's viewport, improving site performance.

M

Metadata
Information about a webpage (e.g., title, description) used by search engines to index and rank your site.

Mobile-First Design
A design approach that prioritizes the mobile experience, ensuring usability on smaller screens before scaling up to larger devices.

N

Navigation Menu
A set of links allowing users to move between sections or pages of a website easily.

No-Code Platform
A tool like Carrd that allows users to build websites and applications without writing code.

R

Responsive Design
A web design approach ensuring your site adapts seamlessly to different screen sizes and devices.

Revision History
A feature in Carrd that allows you to view and restore previous versions of your project.

S

SEO (Search Engine Optimization)
The practice of optimizing your website to rank higher in search engine results, increasing visibility and traffic.

Scroll Effects
Visual animations or transitions triggered as users scroll through a webpage.

Section
A content block in Carrd used to separate and organize different parts of a webpage.

T

Template
Pre-designed layouts in Carrd that serve as a starting point for building your site.

Typography
The art of arranging text on a page, including font style, size, spacing, and alignment.

U

User Experience (UX)
The overall experience and satisfaction a user has while interacting with your website.

URL (Uniform Resource Locator)
The web address used to access your Carrd site or any other webpage.

V

Viewport
The visible area of a web page on a user's device screen, influencing how elements are displayed.

Visual Hierarchy
The arrangement of elements to guide user attention, prioritizing the most important content.

W

White Space
Empty areas around elements on a webpage, used to improve readability and focus.

Widget
An embedded tool or feature, such as a contact form or social media feed, integrated into your website.

This glossary provides a foundational understanding of the terms essential for mastering Carrd and web design. As you continue building your projects, referring back to these definitions will ensure clarity and confidence.

Appendix B: Quick Reference for Shortcuts & Settings

This appendix provides a comprehensive guide to the most useful shortcuts and settings in Carrd, enabling you to work more efficiently and effectively. Bookmark this section for quick access during your website-building process.

1. Keyboard Shortcuts

Streamline your workflow with these essential keyboard shortcuts:

Shortcut	Action
Ctrl + S (Cmd + S)	Save your project.
Ctrl + Z (Cmd + Z)	Undo the last action.
Ctrl + Y (Cmd + Y)	Redo the last undone action.
Ctrl + D (Cmd + D)	Duplicate the selected element.
Delete (Backspace)	Delete the selected element.
Arrow Keys	Nudge the selected element slightly.
Shift + Drag	Move elements in fixed increments.
Ctrl + Click	Select multiple elements.
Esc	Deselect all elements.

2. Frequently Used Settings

Understanding these settings will help you customize your site with precision:

General Settings

- **Page Title**: Set the title of your website, displayed in the browser tab.
  (Settings > General > Title)
- **Favicon**: Upload a small icon that appears in the browser tab.
  (Settings > General > Favicon)
- **Description**: Add a short description for SEO purposes.
  (Settings > General > Description)

Appearance Settings

- **Theme**: Choose a color scheme for your website.
  (Settings > Appearance > Theme)
- **Font Family**: Select a font for your site's text.
  (Settings > Appearance > Fonts)

- **Background**: Customize the background color, image, or gradient.
  (Settings > Appearance > Background)

Advanced Settings

- **Custom Domains**: Connect your domain to the site.
  (Settings > Advanced > Domain)
- **Analytics**: Add tracking scripts like Google Analytics.
  (Settings > Advanced > Analytics)
- **SEO Settings**: Configure metadata and keywords for better visibility.
  (Settings > Advanced > SEO)

---

3. Pro Tips for Efficiency

Quick Element Selection

- Hover over an element and click the **highlighted outline** to select it instantly.

Layer Management

- Use the **layers panel** (accessible in the toolbar) to select and organize overlapping elements.

Responsive Preview

- Click the **device icon** in the editor's top-right corner to preview your site on different screen sizes.

Global Styles

- Apply **Global Styles** to ensure consistency across all elements like buttons, headings, and text.

---

4. Commonly Overlooked Features

Version History

- Revert to a previous version of your project if needed.
  (Settings > History > Restore Point)

Element Visibility

- Control which elements appear on specific devices.
  (Element > Settings > Visibility)

Alignment Tools

- Use the alignment grid for precise placement.
  (Editor Toolbar > Grid View)

---

5. Error-Prevention Tips

- **Save Frequently**: Use the shortcut **Ctrl + S (Cmd + S)** regularly to prevent data loss.
- **Test on Devices**: Always preview your site on mobile, tablet, and desktop screens.
- **Backup Projects**: Export your project file for safekeeping.
  (Settings > Export > Save File)

This quick reference ensures you can find and apply Carrd's most essential tools and features without missing a beat. By mastering these shortcuts and settings, you'll significantly enhance your productivity and your site's quality.

Appendix C: Additional Design Resources & Tools

This appendix provides a curated list of design resources and tools to enhance your projects in Carrd. Whether you're looking for inspiration, assets, or additional functionalities, these resources will help you elevate your single-page website to the next level.

1. Design Inspiration

Awwwards

- **Website**: [www.awwwards.com] (https://www.awwwards.com)
- **Purpose**: Discover award-winning websites for creative inspiration and trending designs.

Dribbble

- **Website**: [www.dribbble.com] (https://www.dribbble.com)
- **Purpose**: Explore design concepts and layouts shared by professional designers.

Behance

- **Website**: [www.behance.net] (https://www.behance.net)
- **Purpose**: View portfolios and projects for inspiration in web design, branding, and more.

2. Stock Images & Graphics

Unsplash

- **Website**: [www.unsplash.com] (https://www.unsplash.com)
- **Purpose**: High-quality, royalty-free images for use in your website designs.

Pexels

- **Website**: [www.pexels.com] (https://www.pexels.com)
- **Purpose**: Free stock photos and videos to enhance visual appeal.

Freepik

- **Website**: [www.freepik.com] (https://www.freepik.com)
- **Purpose**: Download free vectors, icons, and illustrations for your projects.

3. Icons & Fonts

Font Awesome

- **Website**: [www.fontawesome.com] (https://www.fontawesome.com)
- **Purpose**: Access a vast library of scalable vector icons for use in Carrd.

Google Fonts

- **Website**: [fonts.google.com] (https://fonts.google.com)
- **Purpose**: Browse a collection of free, web-friendly fonts to customize your site's typography.

Flaticon

- **Website**: [www.flaticon.com] (https://www.flaticon.com)
- **Purpose**: Find thousands of free icons tailored to your design needs.

---

4. Color Palettes & Generators

Coolors

- **Website**: [www.coolors.co] (https://www.coolors.co)
- **Purpose**: Generate harmonious color palettes to use in your website design.

Adobe Color

- **Website**: [color.adobe.com] (https://color.adobe.com)
- **Purpose**: Create and explore color schemes with Adobe's intuitive tool.

Paletton

- **Website**: [www.paletton.com] (https://www.paletton.com)
- **Purpose**: Experiment with color combinations and schemes for your project.

---

5. Video & Animation Resources

Pixabay Videos

- **Website**: [www.pixabay.com/videos] (https://www.pixabay.com/videos)
- **Purpose**: Free stock videos to add dynamic backgrounds or engaging content.

LottieFiles

- **Website**: [www.lottiefiles.com] (https://www.lottiefiles.com)
- **Purpose**: Access free animations compatible with Carrd for interactive designs.

Animoto

- **Website**: [www.animoto.com] (https://www.animoto.com)
- **Purpose**: Create simple, professional-quality videos for your site.

---

6. SEO & Analytics Tools

Google Analytics

- **Website**: [analytics.google.com] (https://analytics.google.com)
- **Purpose**: Track website performance and visitor behavior.

Moz

- **Website**: [www.moz.com] (https://www.moz.com)
- **Purpose**: Optimize SEO with tools for keyword research and link analysis.

Ubersuggest

- **Website**: [www.neilpatel.com/ubersuggest] (https://www.neilpatel.com/ubersuggest)
- **Purpose**: Free keyword tracking and site performance analysis.

---

7. Additional Tools for Optimization

TinyPNG

- **Website**: [www.tinypng.com] (https://www.tinypng.com)
- **Purpose**: Compress images without losing quality to improve site performance.

GTmetrix

- **Website**: [www.gtmetrix.com] (https://www.gtmetrix.com)
- **Purpose**: Analyze your site's speed and performance metrics.

Canva

- **Website**: [www.canva.com] (https://www.canva.com)
- **Purpose**: Create custom graphics, banners, and social media assets with ease.

---

8. Plugins & Widgets

Embedly

- **Website**: [www.embed.ly] (https://www.embed.ly)
- **Purpose**: Seamlessly embed media content from various platforms into your Carrd site.

Typeform

- **Website**: [www.typeform.com] (https://www.typeform.com)
- **Purpose**: Create engaging forms and surveys to integrate with Carrd.

Zapier

- **Website**: [www.zapier.com] (https://www.zapier.com)
- **Purpose**: Automate workflows and connect Carrd with hundreds of other apps.

This appendix offers all the resources and tools you need to maximize the potential of your Carrd site. Use them to create visually stunning, functional, and optimized single-page websites.

Conclusion

As we wrap up **The Carrd Handbook: Single-Page Websites in a Snap**, you've not only learned the fundamentals of Carrd but also explored advanced techniques and creative applications to make the most out of this powerful no-code platform. From setting up your account and designing visually stunning layouts to enhancing user interaction and optimizing your site for performance, you now have the tools and knowledge to create engaging single-page websites with confidence.

Reflecting on Your Journey

The journey from a concept to a live, functional website can seem daunting at first. However, with Carrd's intuitive interface and the step-by-step guidance provided in this book, you've seen how even the most complex web design challenges can be simplified. By focusing on creativity, clarity, and usability, you've unlocked the potential to build websites that not only look great but also serve a clear purpose.

Key Takeaways

- **Single-Page Simplicity:** You've discovered the power and versatility of single-page websites, ideal for streamlined communication and user engagement.
- **No-Code Empowerment:** With Carrd, you've experienced how no-code tools democratize web design, making it accessible to everyone, regardless of technical background.
- **Endless Possibilities:** Whether it's a personal portfolio, a sales funnel, or a monetized landing page, Carrd offers endless creative opportunities.

What's Next?

The world of web design is constantly evolving, and you're now equipped to adapt and grow with it. Keep experimenting with Carrd's features, stay informed about the latest trends in design, and explore additional tools and integrations to enhance your websites further.

A Final Note of Encouragement

Remember, the beauty of Carrd lies in its simplicity and flexibility. Whether you're a beginner exploring web design for the first time or a seasoned designer looking for a lightweight solution, Carrd offers everything you need to succeed. Every website you create is an opportunity to tell a story, connect with your audience, and achieve your goals.

Your journey with Carrd doesn't end here. With your newfound skills, the possibilities are endless. Embrace creativity, take inspiration from the examples and resources provided in this book, and continue to refine and expand your projects. Your next great website is just a Carrd template away.

Thank you for taking this journey with me, and I wish you all the best in your web design endeavors!